PRAISE FOR *PARTNERSHIP MARKETING*

"Want to extend the power of your brand without being left with the short end of the partnership stick? Read *Partnership Marketing* to get a deep explanation of the intricacies that make for a win-win in a marketing partnership with a roadmap for how to get there."
—*Roy A Young, President, MarketingProfs*

"*Partnership Marketing* is a must-read for any business owner or professional that is looking to take their business to the next level by leveraging marketing partnerships. Ron lays out a practical guide on how to look at your company's assets to create a plan for new or existing partnerships. In addition, this book will help you to make an honest assessment of your current partnerships to ensure you are maximizing the return for your company as well as your partner companies. This is a book that business students should study and partner and non-partner professionals should use."
—*Dan Morton, Director of Strategic Partnerships, Reliant Energy, LLC*

"If this book had been published 20 years ago it would have made my life so much easier in explaining what partnership marketing is to brands! This is the ultimate a-z of partnership marketing and is fully comprehensive but in a very readable way. It has numerous real-life examples of excellent partnership marketing case studies. You can pick it up and read snippets and feel like you have learned something about partnership marketing. You can refer to it for guidance and you can remind yourself of different and varied creative partnership marketing options just by having this book near you and dipping into it. Every brand owner and marketing professional should read it and open their eyes to the fantastic potential, cost-effective options and opportunities that partnership marketing can give them. Don't be without it!"
—*Chris J. Reed, Regional Partnerships Director - Asia Pacific, Partnership Marketing*

"Ron has created a first in the field of partnership marketing. All the essentials of this developing arena are captured here in a concise and illustrative manner. I highly recommend it for all current and aspiring partnership marketers."
—*Mike Burnette, Director of Partnership Marketing, Meredith Corporation*

PARTNERSHIP MARKETING

PARTNERSHIP MARKETING

HOW TO **GROW YOUR BUSINESS** AND **TRANSFORM YOUR BRAND** THROUGH **SMART COLLABORATION**

RON KUNITZKY

John Wiley & Sons Canada, Ltd.

Library and Archives Canada Cataloguing in Publication Data
Kunitzky, Ron
   Partnership marketing : how to grow your business and transform your brand through smart collaboration / Ron Kunitzky.

Includes index.
ISBN 978-0-470-67670-7

   1. Branding (Marketing).   2. Brand name products—Marketing.
3. Partnership.   I. Title.

HF5415.1255.K85 2010   658.8'27   C2010-903735-9

Production Credits
Cover design: Mike Chan
Cover photo credit: ©istock/Gordo25
Interior text design: Natalia Burobina
Typesetter: Thomson Digital
Printer: Friesens

John Wiley & Sons Canada, Ltd.
6045 Freemont Blvd.
Mississauga, Ontario
L5R 4J3

Printed in Canada

1 2 3 4 5 FP 15 14 13 12 11

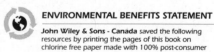

ENVIRONMENTAL BENEFITS STATEMENT

John Wiley & Sons - Canada saved the following resources by printing the pages of this book on chlorine free paper made with 100% post-consumer waste.

TREES	WATER	SOLID WASTE	GREENHOUSE GASES
29	13,139	798	2,728
FULLY GROWN	GALLONS	POUNDS	POUNDS

Calculations based on research by Environmental Defense and the Paper Task Force. Manufactured at Friesens Corporation

To my beautiful wife, Gillian, for being my rock, a wonderful mother to our daughter, and for your unconditional love and support. Our partnership is what makes me strong.

Contents

CONTENTS

Acknowledgments

I WOULD LIKE TO THANK all of the people who took the time to share their experiences and insights in order to make this book possible. Included in that list are former colleagues of mine, clients, industry experts and professionals whose contributions have been extremely crucial to bringing it all together. Your willingness to participate and go above and beyond is greatly appreciated and I couldn't have done it without you. I feel like I am extremely lucky to have such a professional network that spans the globe and is filled with so many people from so many diverse industries. Thanks for being there for me.

I would also like to thank my wife, Gillian, and our daughter, Michelle. You have been a huge support to me and I appreciate it more than you know.

Finally, I would like to thank all the people at John Wiley & Sons in Toronto, especially my editor Karen Milner and her amazing team, including Liz McCurdy, Pam Vokey and Brian Will. It's been a pleasure to work with all of you.

Preface

PARTNERSHIP MARKETING could not be timelier. In today's world of marketing budgets being under constant scrutiny, partnership marketing is now the cornerstone of many marketing plans and programs. The need for collaboration is greater than ever as marketing resources are being slashed, employees are being laid off and cutbacks are being made to existing programs. Employees need to become more creative and do more with less. Brands must rely on each other to leverage their core competencies and they need to create a more prominent role for partnership marketing within their marketing mix.

Partnership Marketing is a guide for business owners, executive leaders and sales and marketing professionals who are looking to improve how they select, develop and manage their marketing partnerships with their partner brands. I believe that every business, charitable organization, association and government corporation can take their organization to the next level by applying the principles and practices of 'smart collaboration' to their particular situation so that they can leverage collaborative marketing programs to help them meet their goals and objectives.

This book is a framework for how you can effectively develop a partnership marketing plan for your brand and, furthermore, develop strategic affiliations that will grow your business and transform your brand by:

- Targeting potential customers when they are most likely to purchase your product
- Launching new product categories outside of what you are known for
- Enhancing your offer to customers by giving them more value than before
- Increasing loyalty for your products and keeping customers loyal for longer
- Locking up a key marketing distribution channel and having exclusive rights to it
- Bringing an aspect of innovation to how customers engage with your product

We begin with a look at what is partnership marketing and how some of the world's most prominent brands have leveraged the strategy to help them achieve the leading positions that they enjoy. We look at how partnership marketing can support and supplement other marketing disciplines and how such activities complement what they are already doing.

Once you are settled in, we analyze the most common types of marketing partnerships and give real examples of how brands are using them. You will have an opportunity to determine which types are most relevant to your business by breaking down the key questions you need to answer before considering them as viable options for your brand. You are not limited to just one type of marketing partnership; you can leverage as many as possible as long as you have what it takes to make them work for you. There have been books written on co-branding, strategic alliances, loyalty marketing and partnering, but my book brings all of partnership marketing together in one set of pages with a focus on the bigger picture of what it can do for your brand.

I then give insight into the assets that you can leverage in your marketing partnerships, like customers, marketing vehicles and your brand, as well as how to measure each type of asset and where to use them to your benefit. If you want to really excel at partnership marketing, you need to know your partner brand very well. In fact, you need to know theirs just as well as you know your own so that you can leverage the right assets in the marketing partnership to meet your goals. The only ways to grow your business without acquiring or merging with another company are to add new customers, increase the number of transactions that existing customers make with you or increase the average transactional value that you are currently getting. You will learn how partnership marketing can foster all of the aforementioned growth strategies and get a glimpse at where you can apply them to your world.

We also examine the foundation of what ultimately makes for a successful marketing partnership—ECP, economic connection as partners. The economic connection as partners and just how much ECP you exhibit in your relationships with partner brands will not only assess whether they see your marketing partnership as valuable to their organization or not, but will provide you with some insight on why most partnerships fail and are doomed even before they are launched. We look at what to seek out in a partner brand as well as what can inevitably go wrong if you associate with the wrong brand, and the ramifications that may result.

I share some case studies from brands that really excel with partnership marketing, with a special focus on why Google is so successful as a result of their partner programs. You may have heard of the famous '4 Ps of Marketing'; this book gets indepth on the 4 Ps of successful marketing partnerships. Later on in the book, I provide you with some of the tools that you will need to get partnership marketing going within your organization so that you can put a plan together and streamline your efforts. In addition, we do an overview of the principles and practices of 'smart collaboration', such as your referral process, engagement strategy and how to train your partners to be more effective when marketing your products and offers.

Finally, we take a look into the future. I give some insights on where I think partnership marketing is heading and what we can expect to see from brands in years to come. I break down some of the current partnership marketing trends that we are seeing in retail, loyalty and product development as well as how small businesses and entrepreneurs will partner with larger corporations.

Every brand sells and markets their products directly, but not every brand leverages partnership marketing. You can try to do it all on your own, yet it's likely easier to spend at least a small part of your time collaborating with others. My goal is to demonstrate the techniques that will get you started on your partnership marketing journey or enhance your existing marketing strategy so that you can create even more success for your organization and your brand.

Introduction

Welcome to the World of Partnership Marketing

WELCOME TO THE WORLD of partnership marketing, where exciting marketing synergies are occurring between organizations large and small, private and public, not-for-profit and for-profit. More than ever before, brands are coming together to create commercial value for themselves and their partner brands by practicing smart collaboration and putting partnership marketing into play, because

1. Partnership marketing enables brands to reach their target audiences.
2. Partnership marketing provides access to underserved markets.
3. Partnership marketing leverages another brand's assets.
4. Partnership marketing strengthens brand image.
5. Partnership marketing builds stronger relationships with customers.
6. Partnership marketing generates new streams of revenue.
7. Partnership marketing increases customer retention.
8. Partnership marketing fosters innovation.
9. Partnership marketing blocks or befriends the competition.
10. Partnership marketing is cost-effective to implement.

Partnership marketing is not an alternative to other marketing strategies. Rather, this type of marketing activity is complementary and purely leverages the assets and marketing vehicles belonging to the members of the marketing partnership in an effort to provide greater value to all. As such, mutually beneficial partnership marketing requires that both partner brands have an established business and complementary core competencies that they can bring to the relationship.

Google, Microsoft, Expedia, Amazon, eBay, Apple, Starbucks, Dell, Best Buy, Facebook, Better Homes and Gardens, and Wal-Mart, to name a few, are the 'category killers' of their respective industries. Why? Because they are brand innovators who have differentiated themselves from their competition to such a degree that it is difficult for other companies to gain market share in the industries that these market leaders dominate. How did these extraordinary companies become the industry stars that they are and what characteristics do they all share?

Loaded questions indeed, but if you dig a little deeper into their businesses, there are clear reasons for their success. Each of these companies has an exceptional product offering and a strong business model to support that offering, coupled with a highly attractive end-customer value proposition. Furthermore, all of the aforementioned companies have built at least a part, if not a significant part, of their business on the principles and practices of partnership marketing, which has enabled them to offer superior products to the market, create long-term distribution opportunities, extend exceptional reach and increase brand awareness on a worldwide level.

Like these companies, developing partnerships with the right partner brands can increase your brand's social and commercial capital and help you to seize more control of your category. You will

- Leverage your core assets and competencies to another business to generate revenue for your business.
- Enter new vertical markets and work with partner brands that will enhance and add value to your existing proposition.
- Stretch your marketing budgets even further to maximize the return on investment you get from your marketing activities.

All of the above are achieved through the practices of smart collaboration and by putting partnership marketing into play.

So what is partnership marketing?
I like to define it as

A collaboration of two or more organizations with the intent to develop a mid-term or long-term marketing program designed to meet each of their respective business goals. The need for a partnership marketing program exists when one organization can accomplish their goals more effectively by leveraging the complementary strengths of another organization pursuing a like customer base.

You can't do it all on your own. If you look closely at some of the brands that have transformed the way we live, you will see that they've had significant help from their marketing partners to get to where they are today.

Brands like eBay need their auctioneers (the public) to provide products and services for auction to users or visitors to their site. They also need distribution to get prospective buyers to visit their site and they need licensing opportunities with cause-related marketing programs to power their online auctions and allow them to leverage their platform in return. That's practicing smart collaboration.

Apple needs wireless carriers to bundle their iPhone products; they need electronics retailers and e-commerce sites such as BestBuy.com to sell their iPhone and iPad products as well as their Mac branded computers. Let's face it, most people buy a smartphone and a service plan from a single wireless carrier like AT&T in the U.S., Rogers in Canada or Vodafone in the U.K. because they provide the voice and data plans as well. Apple owns their own stores and e-commerce websites, but they also want to leverage the reach that the major 'big box' electronics retailers have.

Partnership marketing, using the principles and practices of smart collaboration (discussed in chapter 7), can transform a brand by getting products and services into the hands of consumers via the most cost-effective methods possible, lead to the creation of innovative new products, and can propel a brand and help to sustain its momentum for years to come. Revisiting the example in the previous paragraph, surely all of those wireless carriers have built a business on their own merits, but the question then becomes: As technology continues to develop and newer generations of smartphones and devices enter the market, how relevant are these carriers as brands in the longer term if they don't partner with and make those products available to their customers? I'm not implying that they would disappear altogether if they didn't bundle their services with certain models of smartphones. Rather, I'm wondering what opportunity they would have to increase revenues, market share and profit for their business if they didn't have the most exciting and evolving product lines as marketing partners.

MARKETING PARTNERSHIPS ARE NOT BUSINESS PARTNERSHIPS

How does partnership marketing differ from creating a business partnership where one company owns a stake in the other? Partnership marketing differs because it's not about a company merging with or acquiring another. It's about each company remaining independent and nothing about it constitutes a relationship of partners, joint ventures, fiduciaries or other similar relationships between the parties. Partnership marketing strategies are about connecting for the purposes of supporting each other's marketing objectives—not for the purpose of fusing entire businesses together to make them one. With partnership marketing, it's not about handing over the keys to your company. It's about working with another partner brand to leverage marketing core competencies and assets in an effort to offer new products, acquire new customers or keep existing customers loyal for longer.

Think of it this way: If there is another brand out there that already has your target audience as their customers, and has quite a few of them, then doesn't it make sense to access those customers through that other brand? The other brand makes *your* offer available to *their* customers as opposed to you trying to connect with those customers on your own.

Think of it in the context of Hewlett-Packard and their line of notebook computers. When you buy one and start it up for the first time, you will notice an offer from Microsoft Office encouraging you to try MS Office 2010 for free for sixty days. You can register for the 'free trial offer' via a link right off your desktop. Why does Microsoft do that?

How about asking that a different way—Why wouldn't they? Not only does Microsoft want their customers to upgrade from MS Office 2003, but this is a perfect and cost-effective opportunity to access those very people that they are targeting to meet that objective. Someone who buys a new computer is someone likely to use their software, whether the person is an existing Microsoft customer or a new one, and it's a great way for Microsoft to reach those people; for Hewlett-Packard it's a great value-added offer to their customers.

Microsoft and Hewlett-Packard are not merging or bringing their businesses together; they are simply leveraging a partnership marketing program that helps both brands do more with less investment. That's the power of partnership marketing, and that's what makes partnership marketing different from business partnerships.

MARKETING TO BUSINESSES DIFFERS FROM MARKETING TO CONSUMERS

Business-to-business (B2B) marketing partnerships and business-to-consumer (B2C) marketing partnerships are two entirely different arrangements. Here's how.

With B2B, the End Customer Uses a More 'Formal' Buying Process

Because the end customer purchasing the product is a business as opposed to an individual consumer, it's highly likely that they will go through a more 'formal' buying process when evaluating your proposition, especially if it's not available exclusively from a single partner brand. Companies like Hewlett-Packard sell their business laptop machines through a partner network of value-added resellers who meet the criteria they look for in a partner brand and who can effectively service business customers.

End customers that are businesses are typically more savvy to the fact that they can buy their products through several channels who are looking for their business; a unique or compelling offer featured in one channel only is rare. They are less impulsive than individuals who are shopping online or in a store and want to make that purchase right on the spot.

Partner Motivations Are Different

Your B2B partner or value-added reseller may be promoting many solutions to their customers, perhaps even alternatives to yours, so it's important that you work with them to make your offer extremely competitive and ensure you get the right level of placement or promotion. In B2B, you don't have access to your partner's sales channel and are purely dependent on your partner to resell the proposition on your behalf. In making your offer competitive, you also need to ensure that you are not providing preference to one channel partner over another. If issues of channel conflict were to become known in the industry, you could be regarded less favorably by channel partners or resellers and make the competition appear in a better light by comparison.

HOW YOU CAN ADD PARTNERSHIP MARKETING TO YOUR EXISTING MARKETING MIX

Today's brands are leveraging partnership marketing in many ways. Here are some of the most common uses.

Direct Marketing

- Sharing customer access to discreet channels
- Featuring added-value offers from partner brands
- Offering short-term partner promotions to spike response rates

Sales Promotion

- Collaborating to capitalize on the strength and appeal of partner propositions

- Leveraging stronger promotional messaging
- Holding seasonal and sector-specific activities to gain more sales traction

Advertising

- Demonstrating both brands' might and strength behind a single joint initiative
- Collaborating to create new concepts, products and identities
- Leveraging social media and e-newsletters to create awareness

Branding

- Enhancing brand equity through shared attributes
- Forming deeper customer connections through established brand preferences
- Positioning and aligning to brands with strong core values

Retail

- Leveraging in-store coupons
- Supporting retail loyalty programs and promotions
- Driving awareness through co-op advertising in key marketing collateral

This book will take you through the ins and outs of the most common partnership marketing practices being used by brands today, and provide you with insight on how to apply the concepts and strategies to your brand. Chapter 1 takes a closer look at the different models of marketing partnerships that are, and have been for quite some time, driving business forward for brands.

1

Understanding Partnership Marketing

IN THIS CHAPTER, WE WILL discuss what partnership marketing is, why you should consider it as a marketing strategy, how it can work for you, and ten of the most common partnership marketing models currently being used in business today. As you read through the models, start thinking about which, if any, you are already working with in your company, which are not practical options for your business and which models you are really interested in learning more about to help determine if they just might give your business the marketing edge you have been looking for.

While a model may have been successful for one company, it might not be the best model for your business. So what type of partnership *is* right for you? The answer to that question depends on what you can effectively manage and support given the nature of your business, products and services, budgets and how you typically communicate with existing and prospective customers. At the end of the discussion on each model, I have included a few key questions for you to think through as you begin to create, modify or improve on your marketing strategy.

These are the models that we'll look at:

1. Distribution marketing partnerships
2. Added-value marketing partnerships
3. Affinity marketing programs
4. Affiliate marketing networks
5. Content marketing programs
6. Sponsorship marketing
7. Licensing programs
8. Loyalty marketing programs
9. Co-marketing
10. Store within a store and co-branded stores

DISTRIBUTION MARKETING PARTNERSHIPS

Traditional 'distribution' involves purchasing and then reselling a product or service that a given party within the distribution channel will make a margin on. In a distribution marketing partnership, on the other hand, the primary partner brand is the one that owns the product, has the means by which to get it to the end customer and transacts with the end customer and owns that relationship, while the secondary partner brand is responsible for marketing to their customers, which then become customers of the primary partner brand. The primary partner brand then financially rewards the secondary partner brand for distributing the marketing collateral through a variety of revenue models, as discussed in chapter 7.

Let's look at an example from my time at AOL. AOL, the primary partner brand, entered into a distribution marketing partnership with Best Buy, the secondary partner brand, to display AOL CDs in their stores. With Best Buy providing a storefront distribution channel, AOL was able to offer their product directly to their target market—customers purchasing computers. Best Buy needed to make minimal shelf space available for the product, and AOL had a forum to provide a special offer to Best Buy's customers. The costs were incurred by the primary partner, AOL, who paid for the displays, the CDs, the special customer offers and Best Buy's 'referral' fee for each new customer acquisition.

The partnership is developed between partner brands to leverage marketing capabilities, with the primary partner brand (AOL) taking responsibility for transporting, merchandising and transacting with the customer.

Distribution marketing partnerships typically involve the following:

- Your Partner Brand handles the advertising, emails and other types of customer marketing. It's important to leverage those vehicles to promote your partnership.
- You make unique or compelling offers available to customers as an added value proposition to support and supplement your partner brand's core offering.
- Since you are good at what you do and your partner is good at the business they run, you can leverage what each brand is good at to bring an aspect of innovation to both businesses.
- You develop new products and together plan for product launches, leveraging input from each other from concept to delivery.
- Jointly, you analyze customer data and look for new opportunities to meet wants and needs.
- You work together on primary and secondary market research activities and share your findings with each other.
- You service your customers more effectively by leveraging the insights you might have gained together.

The two main models that can be used for distribution marketing partnerships are bundling and cross-marketing, both of which are explored below.

Bundling

Distribution marketing partnerships are not limited to traditional distribution channels like retailers, e-commerce websites or resellers. Think about the last time you purchased a laptop computer. Did you notice the abundance of flyers packed in the box with special partner-brand offers on products like computer bags and other computer-related accessories? Perhaps you noticed when you set it up for the first time that the desktop was pre-populated with icons offering free trials on high-speed Internet, Skype or other types of VoIP telephone services. This is a form of distribution marketing partnership, where the laptop computer company, for example, Dell, has partnered with a partner brand, Skype, and bundled their offering to drive sales for Skype's products or services by making special offers available to Dell's customers. As a result, Dell generates revenue from Skype by leveraging placement opportunities for Skype via in-box bundles, package inserts and promotion on the computer desktop as opposed to in-store and online distribution marketing partnerships. The benefit to the partner brand, Skype, is that they have direct access to their target audience, who must own a computer to be able to use their service. The benefit of this partnership model to the secondary brand, Dell, is that they not only provide a value-added offering for their customers but generate some sort of revenue from Skype.

Cross-Marketing

In Canada, American Express and RBC Insurance (RBC) have formed a distribution marketing partnership—two competitors coming together to create a new distribution channel. How can that be? While they might both compete in the credit card market, American Express doesn't actually own their own travel insurance product and RBC does. RBC underwrites the American Express travel product so American Express can offer their customers travel insurance marketed as 'Travel Assurance for Emergency Medical Coverage, Trip Cancellation or Interruption, Lost Baggage Coverage and Travel Accident Coverage at americanexpress.ca/travelinsurance.' They may compete in the credit card market, but they certainly can work together when it comes to insurance.

RBC benefits from the partnership by gaining access to the American Express credit card base of customers via American Express marketing the product directly to their customers. (Whether RBC gains access to American Express's entire customer base or simply those individuals who respond to the offer depends on the deal arranged.) RBC delivers the product and American Express brands and markets it. RBC has the opportunity to cross-market the product not only internally within the larger RBC organization, but to new markets as well, by partnering with companies like American Express that make it cost-effective for RBC to market their products and services to a targeted customer base.

Will distribution marketing partnerships work for your company? Here are a few key questions to explore:

- Are the distribution marketing partners that I am considering working with willing to place my offer in their most effective marketing communications vehicles?
- Is the revenue model that I am thinking of presenting to potential distribution marketing partners highly compelling?
- Do I possess the capability to track new customers that are referred to my business by my distribution marketing partner so that I can reward the partner?

ADDED-VALUE MARKETING PARTNERSHIPS

Let's face it—we can't do it all on our own. Most businesses typically possess one core competency and if they are good at what they do, they likely are enjoying high degrees of business success. A baker can bake bread, croissants, pastries and bagels, but can he manufacture toys for kids aged seven to twelve? Not likely. A garage that sells tires and can fit them on your vehicle is probably not all that good at brewing coffee. At least, I don't suspect that they would be. That's OK. Not everyone can be great at everything and a company's strategy should typically focus on their core competencies.

An added-value marketing partnership is one where a primary brand has the ideal product or service to complement a secondary brand with an attractive value proposition, which will allow the primary brand to reach underserved audiences through the secondary brand's ability to target them effectively.

Jason Wagner, President of TrackItBack, a lost-and-found recovery service for mobile devices, keys, luggage and other personal belongings, regularly leverages added-value marketing partnerships to acquire customers for his recovery tracking labels. TrackItBack recently partnered with US Airways to provide their offering to customers of the major airline. "The mechanic was pretty simple," says Wagner. "US Airways sent their customers an email encouraging them to visit TrackItBack.com/US where they could buy TrackItBack recovery tracking labels and would earn free US Airways Dividend Miles with each purchase. For every sale that was made, TrackItBack rewarded US Airways with a commission."

Wagner highlights two main benefits behind the partnership: 1) The brand awareness that TrackItBack received by getting their product in front of the four million US Airways dividend miles members and 2) the sales that this program generated for TrackItBack. TrackItBack leveraged the credibility they earned with the US Airways partnership, and won two additional partnership marketing programs with new partner brands; one is a major loyalty rewards program and the other a leading insurance provider. In this case, the added-value component or 'gift with purchase' is the free US Airways Dividend Miles that the cardholders would receive after purchasing TrackItBack products.

You might be asking yourself, "What is the difference between added-value and distribution marketing partnerships?" The main difference is that added-value marketing partnerships typically offer a true unique value-add to the end customer in the form of a gift with purchase that they can't get anywhere else, while distribution marketing partnerships do not have that component.

Aside from that, there are more similarities than differences between these two types of partnerships. This is because there is a strong component of distribution in developing the added-value marketing partnership. The key differentiator, however, is that while you can have a distribution marketing partnership without offering added value, you cannot have an added-value marketing partnership without an element of distribution.

In the above example, TrackItBack was able to gain access and opportunity to promote and sell their products to a large customer base made available by their partner, US Airways. The distribution component of this partnership involves US Airways making the element of distributing an offer available to TrackItBack through their various customer communications vehicles. The unique offering of the program is the added value offered to US Airways customers to earn free US Airways Dividend Miles for every dollar spent on TrackItBack products. That is perceived as added value by the customer making the purchase and gives them a little something extra from the partner brand that is communicating the offer to them.

1-800-GOT-JUNK?, a primary partner, entered into an added-value marketing partnership with The Beer Store, a secondary partner brand. The offering involved customers that used the 1-800-GOT-JUNK? service with a minimum order receiving a $20 gift card to be used at The Beer Store. The Beer Store included in-store coupons advertising the customer offer, and promoted the offering online on their website. That was all they had to do to earn revenue. For the primary partner, while costs are incurred—in this example, the funding of the $20 gift card—the program is focused on a specific customer target market.

Another example of an added-value marketing partnership that includes the distribution component involves XM Satellite Radio, which equips automobiles like Acura, Lexus, Toyota and GMC with a free three-month introductory trial (i.e., gift with purchase) for customers to try their service in their new car. The partnership allows XM to leverage their relationships with the auto manufacturers to acquire new customers for their service, through the auto manufacturers' distribution channels, and for the auto manufacturers to include a unique added-value product offering with their core product. In this example, if XM Satellite Radio had the same partnership with the auto manufacturers, but without a special unique product offering in the form of a 'gift with purchase,' and ran their standard offer made to any customer who wants to purchase their service, then customers would have to pay for the XM service in full and this would be considered a pure distribution marketing partnership.

In Canada, when you turn on your laptop at Starbucks, you will be greeted with an added-value offer. The retail coffee giant has partnered with Bell to offer free wireless Internet service to anyone who opens a Starbucks-Bell wireless account at the Starbucks website. For customers that are loyal to Starbucks, this is a truly added-value offer; however, for those not committed to the brand, this Internet offering just might make the difference between a customer going to Starbucks or any other coffee-serving establishment. Furthermore, the partnership has the opportunity to meet a further objective for Starbucks. Instead of acquiring new customers, the partnership may be keeping existing customers in the store longer by having them use free wireless Internet service during their stay and gaining more opportunities to increase the number of transactions or quality of the transactions that they make at the counter. As a result, they are increasing the transaction revenue per customer, per store visit. For Bell, this partnership provides access to a discrete customer base (a large segment of Starbucks customers) that is already looking to use the Internet while spending time at Starbucks locations, resulting in a highly targeted marketing opportunity for Bell to potentially target Starbucks customers with offers of their own.

Added-value marketing partnerships can feature a 'gift with purchase' in many forms. It could be a free trial offer beyond what is offered as standard in the market, like free digital HDTV service for a year when you buy a new TV. It could be a unique piece of content, like a video game, screensaver or ringtone for your mobile phone when you buy a new mobile phone, or a unique product, like a free muffin when you buy your coffee or a free T-shirt when you buy a pair of jeans.

Will added-value marketing partnerships work for your company? Here are a few key questions to explore:

- Do I have a compelling and competitive added-value offer to bring to another brand?

- Is the brand that I have identified to partner with a good strategic fit and will the offer being made available increase sales traction for my product?
- As the brand making the added-value offer available, how much money can I dedicate to such an offering while still staying within the company-targeted cost per acquisition (CPA) to acquire a new customer?

AFFINITY MARKETING PROGRAMS

Affinity marketing programs are typically used by associations to create value for their members. An affinity marketing program involves leveraging partner brands where the owner and operator of the program makes special offers available from their partners to their members as a member benefit and the partner brands agree to join the program in exchange for the marketing and promotion to the members that they receive because they made that special offer available.

Unlike an added-value partnership, affinity marketing programs will offer no gift with purchase. Rather, they typically involve a straight discount or perk, and it's possible to get the same discount or perk through other channels.

As outlined below, an affinity marketing program can be used to achieve a number of different business objectives. Its focus can be to retain members of an association (e.g., the American Automobile Association). In other instances, there are organizations that members must join to be in good standing in their profession (e.g., the Canadian Institute of Chartered Accountants) and therefore such a partnership does not focus on retaining members but rather providing a perk to its members. As well, many companies now are joining and, in some cases, creating such programs as part of their employee rewards program.

There are two main types of affinity marketing programs that you can get your business involved in: customized and generic.

Customized Affinity Programs

Affinity programs exist everywhere. From auto associations like the AAA in the U.S. to the CAA in Canada and the AA in the U.K. associations partner with various brands to give discount offers to their members on hotels, car rentals, holiday packages and even prescription drugs. One of the larger membership organizations in the world is the American Association of Retired Persons (AARP) based in Washington, D.C. The AARP offers its more than forty million members discounts on restaurants, entertainment, health products, travel and more. The AARP has partnered with companies like Expedia, where they have created a Travel Center for their members to take advantage of special discounts and targeted offers. Given that 'travel' is a key vertical for the AARP, it's a great way for brands like Expedia to access their member base and make special offers for holidays and excursions. This customized program enables Expedia to gain access to a discrete base of customers within their target audience, with endorsement from the AARP.

Another customized program involves the Canadian Institute of Chartered Accountants (CICA), which offers their 85,000+ member base special discounts from Hertz, Dell Computer, John Wiley & Sons Publishing, RIM (BlackBerry), Starwood Hotels, and Bose to name a few. John Tabone, Manager of Member Value Research for the CICA, says that "the program is not designed to drive revenue or build the brand for the association but to offer members valuable and unique offers on products and services that they are interested in and the program is designed to make members feel like they are getting more from their association."

The CICA, with such a large member base, and given the average income and socio-demographic makeup of their members, is an attractive association for both B2B and B2C brands to want to target. Tabone explains that the CICA is very careful about the brands that they partner with for their affinity marketing program, and has done the research to find out what the members want. When it comes to looking for the right partners, the focus is on partners that will provide highly compelling offers for CICA members, that have national reach and that can easily support the offer in order to create a positive member experience.

Partner brands joining the affinity marketing program and looking to make a special offer available to the members of the program typically will not exchange payments with the owners of the program, but simply fund the offer in exchange for the opportunity to target their members. In some cases, the partner brand may pay to have access to members beyond the planned marketing activities of the affinity marketing program and to be able to email or mail these members directly.

Generic Affinity Programs

There are a number of generic affinity marketing programs that you can consider having your company participate in. Next Jump, as an example, presents companies with a corporate perks program offering employees discounts on merchandise. Next Jump's mission is to be the most valuable, flexible and convenient rewards program worldwide and they currently have more than twenty-five million employees from over 90,000 corporations using their program. Furthermore, Next Jump offers corporations the opportunity to upgrade the platform to a private label version for their employees.

* * *

Both approaches to affinity marketing programs have their benefits. If you choose to create your own, it will be more labor intensive, yet you likely will be able to target offers that are more appealing to your member base. As well, you are much more in control of marketing the program and its offerings to your members and/or employees, because the messaging can easily be integrated into your existing communications and other marketing programs. The benefit of joining a generic affinity marketing program, or 'network' so to speak, is that someone has already done the work for you in acquiring the partner offers and has the turnkey solution ready to go, even if the partner offers are not exactly what your audience is looking for. Such a program still provides a level of value to your member base, yet is clearly not as customized. The decision of which program is right for you will be based on your current objectives, budget and available resources.

Will affinity marketing programs work for your company? Here are a few key questions to explore:

- Do I need to offer my members or employees an affinity program with special perks?
- As a partner brand considering joining an established affinity program, will my message get across if it is grouped together with several other marketing offers? What is the frequency and reach to my member base throughout the year?
- As a partner brand solicited to join an established affinity program, should affinity marketing be part of my strategy? Does my company normally make special offers and discounts available to special groups of potential customers? Do we want to?

AFFILIATE MARKETING NETWORKS

Affiliate marketing networks allow e-commerce or online sellers of goods and services the opportunity to tap into their partner network of thousands of websites with even more potential customers who are visiting those websites. The model for this mass partnership marketing program involves the customer visiting an affiliate website (also known as a publisher), and that website then referring the customer to a partner website (advertiser). If the customer takes a specific agreed upon action, such as filling out a form, making a purchase or subscribing to a service, from the partner website (advertiser), then the partner website pays a commission to the affiliate (publisher) for that customer referral. All of this is carefully tracked online with accurate reporting in real time.

LinkShare (linkshare.com), Commission Junction (commissionjunction .com) and Share a Sale (shareasale.com) are some of the more common online affiliate marketing networks. Specifically, LinkShare provides advertisers with an online marketing channel for finding new customers, by acting as the third party that brings together advertisers and publishers. LinkShare's value proposition, according to their website, is that by choosing LinkShare, you tap into deep online marketing knowledge and experience combined with unique and patented technologies that help turn traffic into sales. What makes affiliate marketing networks interesting is that they cater to virtually any type of business that is communicating with their customers in an online forum. This is because you can join such a program as either a publisher or an advertiser.

Generally, there is no cost for a publisher to join the program. The advertiser, however, has to pay to initiate their programs and usually has to reach minimum targets for transaction revenue or pay a monthly fee to the publisher if that minimum is not reached.

Affiliate marketing networks can be an effective way for online sellers to leverage a group of affiliates to drive traffic to their website. The key is to be sure that you, as the advertiser, are converting a fair number of the visitors that the network drives for you into paying customers, especially if you are paying any additional fees beyond a commission (for not meeting minimum targets) to the affiliate to be in the program. Costs can escalate, resulting in a wasted opportunity and in a negative return on the investment that was made. Keep track of those costs and see if you can have a trial run on the networks before participating over a longer term.

Joining an affiliate marketing network is more of a mass partnership marketing strategy depending on who you choose to go with. As an advertising partner in the network, you are not in control of where your advertisement ends up. You could be placed within any website within the network. You could be a brand with products that target moms and kids, yet the publishers within the network that you join might not target those audiences at all. As a result, the networks can favor the publisher and this could be risky for the advertiser. A brand like Amazon.com, which has a wider target market, tends to have more success in these types of programs. Be sure not to get into a longer-term partnership agreement without testing the waters first.

Will joining an affiliate marketing network work for your company? Here are a few key questions to explore:

- What are the barriers to entry? (Many programs charge entrance and monthly maintenance fees for the advertisers to participate. These costs should be factored into your decision.)

(continued)

- Because of the potentially high fees incurred, as discussed above, is the forecasted CPA in line with company targets? How sensitive is my model, factoring in volume of customer acquisitions?
- Do I have the resources to dedicate to managing this program?
- Will the network offer me a trial run at a reduced cost before I have to make a commitment to the program?

CONTENT MARKETING PROGRAMS

Publishers, online portals, directories, associations, member clubs and online retailers to name a few, need content and a real reason for their customers and members to engage with them. Content marketing programs involve developing attractive content that is highly relevant to your users, readers, members, customers and your target audience such that it might drive a customer action from it, like trigger a purchase. There are two main ways to develop such a program: either create the content yourself or partner with another brand to leverage their content and redistribute it to your customers.

If you visit websites like Yahoo!, MSN and other online portals you will see that much of the content in their channels is pulled from localized sources in their various operating markets like CNN in the U.S., BBC in the U.K. or CBC in Canada. News segments, blogs and stories are published and then redistributed to various portals, communities and Web properties for other readers to enjoy. The truth is that certain storylines will always dominate the interest of online users. So is it really necessary for every publisher or Web property to hire its own writers or bloggers to cast its opinion on a certain topic that is newsworthy, when you can leverage that same content from experts who are already playing in the space? The aforementioned portals do have unique and proprietary content as well, but choose to use a mix of both.

Content marketing exists in TV programming as well. We see more 'product placements' in our TV programming than ever before due to the emergence of personal video recorders like the TiVo, through which you can watch your favorite TV program at a convenient time for you (not necessarily at the specified broadcasted time) and can fast-forward through the TV ads. This has forced advertisers to get creative in placing their products in the actual TV programs. Successful TV programs that will be looking to generate more revenue from their prized asset are primed for content marketing, and it's not all that unusual to see a situation where a significant percentage of the program's script features content from partner brands.

The main questions to consider when determining whether you are looking to build your content in-house or to license or leverage it somehow from others are as follows:

- How will my users interact with my content? Is it static or interactive? Is there a social media element (blogs, podcasts, etc.)?
- What portions of my site will need updating and revising, and how often will I make the changes?
- Do I have the resources in-house to meet the demands of my content strategy or do I need help in this area?
- Are there authorities already in place on the subject matter(s) of my website and can they contribute to what I am doing?
- Can I afford to license or leverage content from others (content owners like publishers, etc.) and do I have reliable prospective licensing partners to choose from?
- Does licensing content from others make sense from a search engine optimization (SEO) perspective? Is the already-written content (which I will be featuring on my site) well optimized?

Based on your answers to the above questions, if you believe that licensing content from partners to leverage their expertise to support and supplement your proposition is the right approach for you, make sure that you

- find out where else the content that you are going to feature on your site will appear;
- are dealing with reliable sources for licensing content and work with experts and proven authors in related fields;

- ensure that the content is well optimized for each topic if it's in fact meant to drive SEO for your website (you can do this by using a content optimization expert with a proven track record);
- are OK with the idea of promoting co-branded content to your users or customers;
- ensure that the content is compatible with the key messages that you are communicating to users of your brand (offline and online), and ensure that it doesn't conflict with or contradict anything that you are currently or already have communicated;
- have a formal agreement with the company that you are licensing from to ensure that all costs, rights, usage and ownership of the content are clearly outlined;
- ask your users/readers if they like the new content that you are featuring and track articles, etc., to ensure that (for the most part) they are enjoyed by those who read them.

Evan Carmichael of evancarmichael.com, a leading website for entrepreneurship, has developed an interesting model around building content for his site and partnering with contributors who author the content for him. According to Carmichael, "One of the big things that helped my company grow is when I stepped away from doing the content creation on my own." Carmichael explains that for a long time, he was writing the content and articles himself, and then realized that he was spending a disproportionate amount of time on content creation, which was distracting him from growing his business. "I then decided to come up with an author contributor program," says Carmichael, "where I went out and started attracting business experts, coaches and practitioners and offered them the opportunity to write for my site. In return for their contribution, I would give them exposure and key placement as an 'expert author.'"

For Carmichael, the model was simple: leverage his expertise in SEO and his ranking as a popular destination for current and would-be entrepreneurs and make it available to business experts to write articles that would be helpful to his users—a partnership where no actual revenue or dollars was changing hands and exposure was purely traded for content. Since the inception of the program, Carmichael has partnered with over five thousand authors who have helped him to build out over eight-four thousand pages of content, ranking him as one of the top destination websites for entrepreneurs in the world. Carmichael calls it a 'win, win, win' partnership where his users win, the authors win and his business wins.

Will content marketing programs work for your company? Here are a few key questions to explore:

- Why do I need content marketing?
- Do I have the skills in-house to create great content and is that how I should be spending my time?
- Do I own content assets that other brands may want to leverage and can I generate revenue from lending those out?

SPONSORSHIP MARKETING

Sponsorship marketing traditionally has been used as a strategy or tactic to drive brand awareness and expose the name of a given brand to the public by affiliating with another brand and their product. We see this type of partnership marketing strategy on a daily basis, at the events that we attend in person, view online or watch on TV.

There are a number of different forums in which you can use sponsorship marketing partnerships. For example, sponsorship was seen at the 2010 Winter Olympic Games in Vancouver, where companies like VISA were positioned as the official credit card, Coca-Cola as the official soft drink, and Sleep Country Canada as the official supplier of bed frames, box springs and mattresses.

Sponsorship marketing has been a part of professional sports for years, not just in North America but all over the world. In the British Premier League, Danish brewer Carlsberg sponsors Liverpool FC and receives placement on all Liverpool communications, including direct placement of their logo plastered on the front of the team jerseys.

Sponsorship marketing is also used in many cause-related marketing campaigns. For example, Home Depot has partnered with Habitat for Humanity and supports volunteer homebuilders in communities worldwide by supplying them with building materials and tools to build homes for low-income families who cannot afford them. Sleep Country Canada, as discussed above, has been able to integrate a cause-related component to their sponsorship partnership. Once the Olympic Games were over, the beds were provided to families in need and charitable organizations across Canada, through Sleep Country Canada's Donated Bed Program.

Sponsorship marketing can be equally effective when applied at the local level. I recall playing ice hockey as a child in Ontario, Canada, and having the Tim Hortons brand featured on my hockey jersey. Taking that a step further, Tim Hortons leverages the endorsement of professional ice hockey superstar Sidney Crosby of the NHL's Pittsburgh Penguins to promote the game of ice hockey across Canada in support of minor league ice hockey programs. This cause-related sponsorship program and affiliation allow for the quick-service restaurant to further integrate within the communities in which their businesses operate. They benefit from the association with Canada's national sport at the grassroots level and affiliate their brand to hockey families from coast to coast.

What we have seen in recent years is that sponsorship marketing (when done through smart collaboration) can do a lot more than just create awareness. It can increase reach, drive traffic, support and supplement a community initiative, drive sales and commercial activity, and ultimately, enrich a brand's social and commercial capital.

Will sponsorship marketing work for your company? Here are a few key questions to explore:

- How do sponsorship programs fit with other advertising that I am already doing?
- Can I afford to enter into a sponsorship agreement and is that the best way for me to use my available budget?
- Are the sponsorship programs that I am considering going to reach the target audience that I am after?

LICENSING PROGRAMS

In 2008 the worldwide licensing industry was worth approximately US $170 billion in retail, with the U.S. generating approximately $110 billion (approximately $5.8 billion in royalties) and Europe $34 billion (sources: EPM Communications for retail and LIMA for royalty information). The U.K. brand licensing industry is worth around £7 billion in retail and £368 million in royalties (source: Licensingpages, with reference to LIMA and EPM figures). If you have a base of customers that typically adore your brand and associate themselves with it as part of their persona, like the loyal fans of a given British Premier League Football team or National Hockey League team or Major League Baseball team, and they are willing to wear that brand on their sleeve, then you likely have a brand worth licensing.

Customer loyalty is hard to build, especially in the hypercompetitive world we live in today, and consumer admiration, passion and affiliation with a brand is almost impossible to create from nothing. What's even more impressive is that the dedication that certain people have is often undeserved or unsubstantiated. Look at the passion for the NHL's Toronto Maple Leafs, who have not won a Stanley Cup Championship since 1967 and have the largest professional ice hockey following in North America as well as the highest valuation of any NHL club. How about the Chicago Cubs, who have not been crowned World Series Champions in over one hundred years, yet whose following extends well beyond 'Wrigleyville' to across the U.S. and around the globe, with one of the most loyal fan bases in all of Major League Baseball. It's hard to believe that such underperformers would attract such a strong and loyal following and hold on to it for more than a lifetime in some cases.

Having passion for a product is highly emotional and hard to pin down, so if your product has earned it, then capitalize on it. Some brands are doing this by working with partners or experts in other areas to extend their offering beyond their core products by licensing products and services and accumulating assets to offer their fans or customers.

It used to be that if you were a fan of the National Football League's New York Giants, you could demonstrate your support and adoration to others by wearing a replica of their team jersey and baseball-style hat. Nowadays, you can purchase table lamps, armchairs, T-shirts, coats, jackets, pillows, sheets, rugs, doormats, barbecue accessories and over one hundred different varieties of their team baseball-style hat! Affiliating with brands that are adored can only result in a great opportunity to generate revenue for partners who manufacture and distribute the aforementioned products and it's the power and loyalty for those brands that help them sell even more and for more profit than the same non-branded product.

Popular weight-loss brand Weight Watchers has a line of digital scales that is produced for them by Conair (Conair licenses the Weight Watchers name and puts it on the scales). Leveraging the Weight Watchers brand provides Conair with access to a massive base of Weight Watchers members that they normally would not have access to and can even get them extra shelf space in retail stores. Both Weight Watchers and Conair have a dedicated page on their respective websites and the affiliation with the brand allows them to keep even more market share away from their competitors.

If you have a brand with a very strong following, you can develop a series of uniquely branded products that will appeal to your customers via a licensing program that typically consists of a three-way relationship encompassing the following players:

1. Brand owner/licensor

   You are the brand custodian. You own the trademarks for the Guinness Brewing Company, Boston Red Sox baseball club or Ford Motor Company and its products and services are your intellectual property.

2. Manufacturer or distributor/licensee

   You are the manufacturer or distributor that sells products to retailers or e-commerce websites where you have obtained the rights from the brand owner or licensor to do so. For example, you are a manufacturer of bottle openers and you have obtained the rights to Budweiser; you sell bottle openers with the Budweiser brand on them to retailers.

3. Retailer/e-commerce site
   You are the channel that ultimately sells the product to the end consumer. In some cases, retailers can be the licensees as well, especially if they are large multinationals with major buying power and distribution, such as Wal-Mart.

According to Samantha Taylor, an expert in licensing programs and licensing manager for Mattel in Canada, there are three key factors to look for when assessing the right partner for a licensing agreement.

1. Market opportunity
   An assessment must be done to determine the value of the product category in your geographic market. Is there a gap? Who else is competing for that product category in that geographic market? Taylor encourages you to select strong licensing partners who have experience in a given geographic market so they can capitalize on the market opportunity where possible.

2. Right fit and strategic partnerships
   Does the licensee understand what your business is about? Are they able to develop a product that will speak to the consumer in the same way that your brand does?
   Which prospective licensee has the right fit for the particular brand you are looking to license? For Taylor, the answer to these questions and therefore the approach would be different when considering licensing opportunities for one brand versus another, as it is not likely that one licensee would be able to support them effectively across all of these brands.

3. Your licensees' understanding of the market you are working in
   If you are looking to use a U.S. licensee, how do they intend to operate in Canada? Do they have a local representative and relationships with the

buyers? In the case of Canada, do they have an understanding of the two-language (English and French) requirements of the Canadian market?

Similarly, a licensing strategy can be used by brands who sell to businesses as opposed to consumers. This is very common with startup software companies who develop the proprietary code for a given software application, but want larger, more established software giants to sell and market it to their customers for them. They too would have to be selective in who they partner with to ensure that the licensee has access to the right customers and could effectively get it into channel. For them, it's less about extension into new product categories and more about how they plan to get their core product to the target audience.

Overall, Taylor's approach is to look for market leaders in certain product categories, or licensees who are able to show a fresh and new approach to product development. The objective is to have your licensed products on shelf appear as an extension of your core products, like a child's backpack is to a doll, for example. The customer is buying a branded product and expects the same level of product quality across all categories. Therefore, finding the right licensee who can truly exemplify the brand is critical.

Will licensing programs work for your company? Here are a few key questions to explore:

- Do I have a brand that my customers adore?
- What kind of licensed products can be created for my brand?
- Have I established the criteria that describe the type of licensing partner I want to have?

LOYALTY MARKETING PROGRAMS

I like to define a loyalty marketing program as "a partnership that will help you to attract customers, build frequency of interaction, increase transactional value and therefore revenue and, ultimately, reduce customer acquisition costs."

Tim Moulton has extensive experience building loyalty marketing programs. Moulton believes that a partnership with a loyalty marketing program is a strong marketing tool that enables partners in the program to align brand power to better understand customer segments, product preferences and purchasing behavior. Most program partners provide an established membership base ideal for brands like yours to target them as customers. The value proposition and marketing vehicles that fuel programs allow partner brands to influence customers to choose their brand more often and spend more when they transact, and provide meaningful promotions and communications when positioning new products. These programs also allow partner brands to speak directly to their customers for ad-hoc promotions enabling up-sell or cross-sell opportunities.

The two main types of loyalty marketing programs that a business can implement are

1. a proprietary program, which focuses on an in-house program that may have some coalition partners that directly partner with the issuing business.
2. a coalition program, which involves a strategic partnership with an existing program such as a reward miles program;

A proprietary program design is a very flexible structure that allows the program team to align with strategic partners that complement the value proposition to help increase new customer acquisition. These partners may be vendors or participating strategic partners (e.g., Lays 'ChipTrips' and Marriott).

The pros of a proprietary program center on owning the assets and marketing collateral (the materials used to promote the program). In this case, the brand will own the customer data, brand and program structure. This flexibility allows a retailer, for example, to be nimble, timely and effective with their promotions and program offers. Costs are incurred only when the customer feels value through redemption of points or whatever 'currency' is to drive the program (usually between one percent and three percent return). If the program is executed properly, the majority of program costs should be passed through to vendors, program partners and, in some cases, the franchisees.

The cons of a proprietary program include the time it takes to educate the customer base and enroll customers to a critical mass; it can take up to three years to have a mature enough program to affect wall-to-wall sales in a meaningful way.

The industry is trending towards proprietary programs. Many consulting companies are entering the market to facilitate these types of program constructs. For many years, brands have concentrated on the one-to-many marketing communications strategies, focusing on mass media, but now they are shifting to a one-to-one strategy. Customer centricity and customer-centric retailing are the new buzzwords and many businesses realize this is an effective natural way to sustain or increase sales as well as provide protection/differentiation over the large competitors and new hypermarket structures. By providing relevant, timely offers to customers that want them, brands are realizing that they can protect their market positions and grab a measurable share of household spending at the same time.

The reasons for this shift are many. In the coalition structure, businesses do not own or have access to program information other than basic program reporting and standardized promotional tools. This makes it difficult for their marketing and CRM (customer relationship management) departments to truly understand their customers and drive partner offers that are more relevant to them. By moving to a proprietary loyalty program, companies do away with programs that incur significant costs (between one percent and four percent) and offer little ownership of or return on collateral. Proprietary loyalty programs are a significant initiative and touch every aspect of a business's operation from marketing and store operations to MIS (management information systems) and vendors. As a result of the impact on the business an education or change management strategy is required to be sure all stakeholders are aligned.

Before deciding to undertake a loyalty marketing program, a company should consider brand fit, alignment of the coalition partners (do we share in similar customer bases?) and cost impact. It is essential to develop a measurement plan—consisting of the metrics that you are going to measure, such as change in sales, number of new customers or transactions per customer—before you launch your program and cross-promote with other partners. An exit plan is helpful to ensure you may divest your partner relationships and wind down the awards program while maintaining customer base loyalty when the loyalty marketing program no longer provides a measurable impact.

Components of a Successful Loyalty Marketing Strategy

A successful loyalty strategy includes six key components. To better understand these components, let's look at how AIR MILES has been able to successfully apply these factors to their loyalty program. AIR MILES is a reward program that offers its members the opportunity to earn points ('reward miles') from the purchase of everyday products and then to redeem those reward miles for valuable merchandise. As the largest reward program in the world, AIR MILES has built a large partnership network to provide its users with a number of opportunities to earn reward miles and with compelling offers to convert the miles into exciting rewards.

1. Strong value proposition

   A clear, strong value proposition and message is necessary to attract people to the program. Many programs tailor specific messages to customer segments or individuals that promise them an award for their spending habits (a discount or currency that can be used for product), special promotional offers (customer recognition days) and unique vendor promotions. There are many types of rewards that can be issued to customers to influence behavior, such as a currency, point systems (proprietary or coalition) or a discount program that enables customers to track their behavior and eventually earn a meaningful reward. As noted above, AIR MILES offers its members reward miles when purchases are made at participating stores (AIR MILES Sponsors). Members can then make purchases with these reward miles for various types of merchandise from AIR MILES participating partners (AIR MILES Partners).

2. Customer acquisition

   How will you acquire members to join the program? What type of messaging will be distributed to inform consumers or businesses that such a program exists? How can the registration process be made as hassle-free as possible to encourage people to join? You can join the AIR MILES Program on their website (or by finding a link to the AIR MILES website when visiting the site of one of the AIR MILES Sponsors), by completing an application that takes no more than five minutes to complete.

3. Customer tracking tool

   A company requires a tool to identify their customers at each touch point, such as a membership card or some kind of unique identifier. AIR MILES uses a membership card to track behavior. Members simply must present their membership card at participating AIR MILES Sponsors to collect their points. The card number is then used as the member's unique identifier. AIR MILES also has partnered with some credit card companies, where miles are earned with each credit card transaction. This is another tool used to track customer activity.

4. CRM infrastructure and program measurement strategy

   A solution to capture the data (i.e., data warehouse) at the various customer touch points, such as the point of sale and online, is the backbone of the program. Data is the key when building and running a loyalty marketing program. The data allows the program to identify and track active customers, behavior and brand preferences. The data is the most significant asset to the company running the program and the vendors participating in the program when it comes to identifying key trends and to measuring program success via flags and reports.

5. Communications plan

   A loyalty marketing program should be as much a part of a brand's communication strategy as catalogs, flyers and e-communications. The more sophisticated a business becomes with their data capture and analytics, the more relevant and tailored their programs can become in targeting individual customers. For example, AIR MILES encourages their coalition partners to promote their program through their marketing vehicles.

6. Exit plan

In the event that the program does not drive the behavior desired by the business or the program plateaus, it is important to have a way to eliminate the program with minimal customer and vendor impact. Without this component the program becomes a margin-chopping cost of doing business.

Businesses that implement a loyalty marketing program seek to better understand their customers so they may acquire more customers, maintain their base of customers, understand their customers' decision-making methodology and life cycle, and provide meaningful offers and messages that build an affinity and solidify the long-term commercial relationship with the customers.

> Will loyalty marketing programs work for your company? Here are a few key questions to explore:
>
> - Does my company/business need a loyalty marketing program to achieve its customer acquisition and retention objectives?
> - Do I want to develop the program on my own and attract coalition partners and issue my own reward currency, or do I want to partner with a major loyalty marketing program provider?
> - If I were to develop a proprietary program, would it be worth my while to outsource the data warehousing and management?
> - If I were to offer a loyalty marketing program to my existing customers, what sort of impact would it have on my business?

CO-MARKETING

Co-marketing is a type of marketing partnership where two or more companies create and jointly develop a new product, service or brand and then use joint marketing efforts to promote it to the target audience.

A few years ago, I worked with Cardinal Watches on a program to create new products for their company using a co-marketing strategy. We were able to gain interest in a concept we developed for Pearl Drums called the

'Tymekeeper.' With the purchase of selected Pearl Drums Kits, customers received for free a value-added gift pack worth approximately $150. The Tymekeeper included a stainless steel watch branded with Pearl-Cardinal, mini flashlight, drum key, carrying case and Pearl-branded lanyard. The flagship in the gift pack was the stainless steel watch featuring NiteLite technology, a rugged nylon strap and a belt clip making it ideal for drummers. The advertising copy on the in-store marketing vehicles read, "Next to a great kit, the most important thing a drummer can have is The Gift of Good Time, so Pearl Drums and Cardinal Watches have teamed up to give you just that."

Obviously, much more goes into developing a new and unique product through a co-marketing relationship than goes into a couple of partner brands engaged in partnership marketing to market an existing product. After deciding on the product, the partner brands have to decide who is sharing and owning costs from either side and how they are going to market to customers. In the Pearl-Cardinal example, it was decided that since Pearl was the brand offering the Tymekeeper as the value-add to their customers who purchased a new drum kit, they would pay for the cost of the gift packs. To benefit from economies of scale, they ordered a decent number of them. Cardinal Watches would pay for the retail point-of-purchase display units that would be used to advertise the Tymekeeper in music stores as well as the Tymekeeper website. The brands decided to split the cost of advertising in certain music and drum magazines for additional promotion. It is essential to draw out the estimated costs as well as the contribution each partner brand is expected to make to ensure that all is accounted for in advance of finalizing the partnership, as this is critical to ensuring the program meets both partners' objectives.

Pennsylvania-based snack company Herr's is another user of co-marketing. They have formed a relationship with another Pennsylvania-based brand called Heinz to produce a product called Herr's Heinz Ketchup Potato Chips, where the two highly trusted brand names leverage each of their core competencies to develop a new product for the snack food category. The goal is to achieve twice the market impact and twice the customer pull, and to create a highly compelling value proposition that will give the snack company—Herr's—an advantage in their category and provide Heinz with a new marketing vehicle with front-and-center placement on the packaging and messaging that tells the customer that Heinz tomato ketchup is one of the key ingredients in the new product, making it even better than before.

Companies like American Express have partnered with big-box retailers like Costco, where they have created a Costco-American Express credit card. This gives American Express the opportunity to offer exclusive incentives to Costco members, incentives like cash cards, special promotions and discounts. In turn, Costco markets the card to members, helping American Express acquire new customers. Costco benefits from their preferred partner status with American Express, as the exclusive provider of the Costco credit card.

Nike has partnered with Apple to develop the Nike-iPod sport kit. This wireless sensor, inserted beneath the insole of your Nike shoe, turns your iPhone or iPod into your own personal trainer by sending information to your Apple device. What's great about it is that you can track your time, distance, pace and calories burned during your workout. When you are back at your computer, you can sync your iPod or iPhone to transfer your workout data to iTunes and nikeplus.com, where you can evaluate performance history, set goals and even challenge others to a virtual race.

Will co-marketing work for your company? Here are a few key questions to explore:

- Do I have an idea for a product that I would like to create, but don't have the missing ingredient to create and develop it?
- Is there another brand out there that would provide credibility and be able to co-market the new product that I want to create?
- If I am going to create this new product, what benefits or product features will it have that my existing products do not have, and what impact will it have on my business and my partner's business?

STORE WITHIN A STORE AND CO-BRANDED STORES

A store within a store is a partnership in which one retailer leases a section of their store to another brand to run another retail operation from. This agreement is popular among gas stations and supermarkets. Bookstores like Borders have leased space to Seattle's Best and have created Seattle's Best Cafes in many of their store locations to give book shoppers a place to sit and enjoy a beverage while reading a book.

A brand can leverage store-within-a-store partnerships to cost-effectively enter new markets and gain access to footfall traffic. This is exemplified by Wal-Mart, which has allowed McDonald's franchisees to open and operate restaurants within their stores. Or Lowe's hardware stores, which often feature Subway restaurants. In 1995, Starbucks formed a partnership with Chapters bookstores to grow the brand in Canada and since then, riding on the success of the store-within-a-store program initially launched, they have opened more than seven hundred company-operated stores.

Rocky Mountain Chocolate Factory and Cold Stone Creamery operate co-branded stores, which differ from store-within-a-store relationships. The stores are fully co-branded to both brands and marketed as such. We have seen this with FedEx and Kinkos; UPS and Staples used the co-branded store strategy to create a presence together in China.

The store-within-a-store and co-branded store concepts are specific to retail markets and offer multiple benefits, including the ability to share costs in an effort to lease prime real estate and the ability to cross-market products from one brand to the other on-site, as well as the targeting of incremental traffic that might be there for another purpose.

Will creating a store within a store or a co-branded store work for your company? Here are a few key questions to explore:

- Do I want to partner with another brand to share my retail space?
- Am I looking for retail space and don't want to incur the associated expenses on my own?
- If I were to partner with a brand to co-brand a store, which brands would best supplement my brand?

∙ ∙ ∙

This chapter outlined the various types of partnership marketing programs that are commonly used today. These partnerships can be applied in different ways and can overlap each other, with more than one form of marketing partnership being featured in the partner relationship. Chapter 2, Leveraging Partnership Marketing Assets, will show you that you may have more to leverage in a marketing partnership than you think.

2

Leveraging Partnership Marketing Assets

IN ORDER TO POSITION your company to be able to create successful marketing partnerships, it is fundamental that you complete an inventory of your partnership marketing assets and have a full understanding of them. What partnership marketing assets do you own and what are they worth to your company and/or a prospective partner? It is equally important to assess what marketing assets you lack as this likely will be a key attribute you will be looking for in potential partner brands you would like to form partnerships with.

It is essential that you have a great knowledge of your partnership marketing assets because there in itself is the 'sweet spot' that your partner brand will be looking for and want to leverage. It is these assets, and more specifically the quality of such assets, that will play a critical role in determining whether the partner brand will want to partner with you. The process of listing out all of your partnership marketing assets and placing a value on them can be a very time-consuming exercise; however, it is the only way for you to uncover the true substance of your value proposition and expose it to your partner brands.

To understand what it is you can offer a partner brand—and of equal importance, what a partner brand can offer you—it is important for you to take the
time to do this analysis, whether on your own or by hiring a third party to
work on it with you.

What are partnership marketing assets? Simply put, they are all of the
qualities that make up your company—that make your products/services
unique in some way, your distribution channel(s) effective for the products/
services you sell and your customers unique because they are of either a specific demographic or behavior or are appealing because you target the mass
market. They are any and all of the variables that have helped to promote and
build your business, to make your company successful and one that a partner
brand would want to leverage from you in a marketing partnership, as you
would from them.

Partnership marketing assets can be classified into three main categories
as summarized below, which further break down into subcategories that are
discussed in this chapter:

- Your brand
- Audience and customers
- Marketing vehicles
  - Online and digital marketing vehicles
  - Traditional marketing vehicles

YOUR BRAND

Whether you sell a product or service or both, you need to think of your
brand in the context of how you and your partners can generate revenue from
it. As discussed in chapter 1, licensing your product is one way well-known
brands can generate revenue, although it's not an option for all businesses.
Given that their brands are less valuable than heavily branded companies,
small and mid-sized businesses need to become more creative when it comes
to leveraging their brand in exchange for lead-generating opportunities or
some kind of goodwill as opposed to revenue. This may not immediately help

your bottom line, but over time those warm leads can turn into some great revenue-generating opportunities.

Brands associated with high perceived value can be leveraged in partnership marketing activities to generate revenues for all parties. McDonald's likes to supplement their already strong brand by associating their restaurants with what they expect to be upcoming blockbuster films. For the release of the film *Avatar*, the popular chain of quick-service restaurants partnered with Academy Award–winning director James Cameron and Twentieth Century Fox to create an interactive game for the movie. The game reveals the world of Pandora, the planet where the movie is set, and it's done up in style with high-resolution graphics and three-hundred-and-sixty-degree views. The game is called PandoraQuest and is accessible on McDonald's websites. McDonald's used popular social media sites like Twitter to drive traffic to the game.

Essentially, your brand is the engine that drives your company. True, there are huge benefits to branding and doing a great job of branding your company, products and value proposition, but if we are looking at this from the partnership marketing perspective, it's about *leveraging* the brand. If you have done a great job with your branding strategies and you have a well-recognized brand with lots of potential, a true point of difference and high levels of awareness and relative strength, then you have something to leverage as a partnership marketing asset.

Companies with a brand that is perceived or viewed to be worth something are in a position where prospective partner brands will want to leverage their brand and associate with it. In some cases, a brand can be presented as a leveragable partnership marketing asset. If you are considered an industry leader, then just having your brand appear next to another brand could very well provide them with credibility, which means that you are bringing a lot to the table. For example, if you have twenty-five thousand active and paying customers and have the opportunity to partner with a company in a loyalty marketing program whose brand reaches over five million customers, then just being seen to be working with them provides credibility to your brand.

Brands with a strong brand identity, like Apple, Coke, Google or Toyota, are iconic and have taken on a life and personality of their own. Most brands don't reach that level, and you don't need to be one of them to successfully partner with another brand; all you need is that your company has other assets that form a basis or reason for the partner brand to want to partner with you.

You can have success in leveraging your brand in a marketing partnership if your brand:

- Has a well-recognized name
  Brands like Cadbury, Mercedes-Benz, Starbucks and Black & Decker are well recognized and very established. They are the kinds of companies that many brands would want to partner with, so incoming requests for their participation in partnership marketing programs likely exceeds their outgoing calls. Brands with a well-recognized brand name have power and control of their categories and influence over customers. They are well established because they adhere to their promise; they consistently deliver a price/value proposition that consumers expect to receive and they rarely let their customers down. Such brands need no introduction, no history or sales pitch as to why they make for an attractive partner with another partner brand. Well-recognized brands are received with open arms and are always considered to be an opportunity for partnership just on their name alone.

- Can be private labeled
  Private label brands often are referred to as 'our own brands' or 'store brands,' as in the case with the popular U.K.-based retailer Marks & Spencer, who have created their own brands for categories like clothing and food and compete exceptionally well vis-á-vis strongly branded products. Another example is Trader Joe's in the U.S. with over three hundred locations nationwide that sell food products that are manufactured for them by another company and sold under the Trader Joe's brand.

Business services like web hosting and data recovery are often private labeled to the brand that is selling them to business customers. For example, web designers will often host their clients' websites under their brand name because they own the client relationship, yet it's not the web designers that are actually operating the website hosting service on the back end—it's their partners that are doing so.

Wal-Mart (the world's largest retailer) sells a whole host of popular, well-recognized brands, yet they also leverage their reach and market share to offer private label brands as well, like Great Value and Sam's Choice, named for Sam Walton, their famous founder.

Not every brand can be private labeled or can successfully develop a new private label brand. You need to be trusted, have a strong proposition and offer exceptional value for the prices you are charging to compete with those well-known brands. Those not so well recognized may do better to focus on the benefits of their product and revenue model to entice partner brands to work with them.

- Lends itself to brand extension

  Can your brand be leveraged to create new products? Michelin is a well-known brand for tires that you would find on your automobile, but they also own a series of travel guides that list hotels and restaurants and award Michelin Stars as a ranking system. Adidas has always been known for sportswear, yet they also have extended into other product categories, such as deodorant. Dell was once just about computers, but in recent years offers servers and other hardware like Digital TVs for sale under the Dell name. This is not about line extension of an existing product within the same product category, like how Coca-Cola offers Cherry Coke or Diet Coke, but about the brand's ability to create new products and leverage their brand by licensing it or partnering in one form or another to launch new products.

If your brand isn't well recognized, cannot be leveraged to private label products from another manufacturer or cannot lend its name to create brand extension, you still could partner with other brands. It's just that your brand is not a partnership marketing asset that can be leveraged in your marketing partnership. More casual arrangements for lesser-known brands are quite common. For example, physiotherapists partner with physical trainers to refer business to each other. I've seen cases where local artists hang paintings at their local coffee shop and leverage the retail space as a showroom for their work and an opportunity to sell their art. Finally, I was in a local toy shop the other day and saw some flyers for a kids' birthday party planner. This is a somewhat less formal marketing partnership, but it seemed, nonetheless, to be quite effective and well aligned to benefit both small business owners.

How to Assess Recognizability of a Brand

- The brand can be associated with a certain tagline, logo or product attribute (e.g., McDonald's 'I'm Lovin It')
- The brand is considered a leader in their product category, as determined by market share, sales and distribution
- The brand has been established for quite some time, be it months or centuries

---

AUDIENCE AND CUSTOMERS

Your audience and customers are made up of a group of people or businesses that your products and services appeal to. In the case of consumers, they are of a certain age group or gender or exhibit a type of behavior that has them wanting to connect to your brand to fulfill a need or want that they have. In the case of a businesses, the customers are part of a given industry, have a business of a certain size and manufacture certain types of products or services and, as a result, would find your proposition attractive and want to buy from you. Customers are often known as buyers, clients or purchasers, yet it's all the same thing: a given party (business or consumer) that buys and transacts with you on a regular basis and is engaged with your brand and products as a result.

In August 2009, GM ran a program with eBay Motors for their two hundred and fifty dealerships in California whereby car buyers were able to negotiate with dealers online at co-branded websites like gm.ebay.com as well as eBay's main site without ever having to set foot in a showroom. The move certainly gave credibility and revenue-generating opportunities to eBay Motors, as they were now associated with a major automaker like GM. For GM, eBay provided the platform to run their program, but more importantly, GM was able to access a large base of eBay users and customers that were already on eBay looking for deals without having to drive all that traffic themselves. It marked the first time that a Detroit auto company used an online auction site for new car sales.

In November 2009, Google announced that they were going to offer free Wi-Fi Internet access at major U.S. airports throughout the holiday season. The partnership with Boingo Wireless allowed Google to provide Wi-Fi to travelers in forty-seven airports. Microsoft and JiWire announced a program around that time as well, teaming up to launch free Wi-Fi at thousands of participating airport and hotel hotspots in exchange for one search on the company's new Bing search engine (Source: MarketingVox.com, August 2009). Online brands like Google and Microsoft's Bing search engine make money when people use their search engines to search the Internet. By offering free Wi-Fi in airports and hotels, Google and Microsoft were able to reach mass volumes of travelers and have users interact with their brands during their travels. Obviously, with the holidays being a peak travel period, it's a great time to target users who may have never used the search engines before, to teach them more about the product and to have them potentially become loyal users of such services in the future. Those airports provided Google and Microsoft with the opportunity to target and access travelers in general as well as a large audience of holiday travelers who could be searching for last-minute deals on hotels, car rentals or restaurant reservations in their destination city.

Well-Defined Target Audience and Customers

Do you know who your audience and customers are? Do you know if they buy from you because they exhibit a certain behavior, like customers of B&Q in the U.K., Home Hardware in Canada or Lowe's in the U.S., who are undertaking a renovation at home or have a do-it-yourself project on the go and need tools and some paint to complete the job? Is your brand one that sells learning software to kids aged seven to eleven and are your customers primarily moms? Knowing who your audience and customers are is a very important thing to get a handle on if you want to leverage them as a partnership marketing asset. Brands will want to know what your customer profile looks like, which is essentially a description of the demographic and behavioral characteristics that make up your customers. Whether they are consumers or businesses, they must be defined.

Regular Frequency of Interaction

How often do your customers or audience communicate with your brand? Do they visit your website three times a week or is it once or twice a year? Do your customers have regular orders in place for your products or services or do they just call you up or visit your website when they need something? Grocery store supermarket chains like Safeway see their customers about once a week in North America, yet likely would see them closer to three times a week in the U.K., given customer shopping frequency there. It's important to identify how often your customers buy from you and what the nature of customer interaction is for your given category. If you are a mobile phone service like T-Mobile, you may want to sign up customers for a thirty-six-month service contract, giving you at least three years of interaction with your customers by way of monthly billings and other communications. A brand like 1-800-GOT-JUNK? is likely to transact with their customers for residential waste removal services only once or twice a year. The frequency of interaction is important in assessing the value of your customer and audience relationships.

Volume or Size

Another important asset is your database of customers. How large is it? If you are a company with four hundred customers and want to grow by fifty percent the following year, then engaging in a partnership with a brand that only has three hundred customers is not going to help you reach your goal. That would mean that you would need to convert sixty-six percent of their customers into your own, which would be a pretty difficult thing to accomplish in most cases. Knowing how many customers you have is crucial to leveraging them as an asset in a marketing partnership, as the volume or size will determine if the partner brand can meet their objectives and realize a great opportunity by partnering with you.

Without knowing what your customers look like, the frequency of interaction you have with them and how many you have, you cannot leverage them as a partnership marketing asset. Every business that is generating sales has customers, but to leverage them in a marketing partnership, you need to define what your audience and customers look like and what your reach is. Without it, a given partner brand will not be able to determine if the focus they place on your brand will provide the right return on investment or may prove an expensive mistake with a high opportunity cost associated with it.

How to Identify the Target Audience and Determine Frequency of Interaction and Size of Customer Base

AUDIENCE

- The partner brand should have similar customer profiles to your brand, i.e., age, gender, income, lifestyle, life stage, behavior, hobbies, interests, likes and dislikes, needs and wants.
- Ask your prospective partner brand who they appeal to. What is their audience and how and when do their customers buy their products?
- Make sure that if you are engaging with a program to market online only, you understand where their traffic is coming from. If you are targeting customers in Australia, then be sure to partner with a brand that targets the Australian market.

(continued)

Frequency of Interaction and Size of Customer Base

- Get an idea of how often they interact with customers and how.
- Be sure to understand how many customers the partner brand has or how much traffic they get on their website.

MARKETING VEHICLES

You can't access a brand and its customers without marketing vehicles. Your marketing vehicles are what you use to execute your marketing strategy and they deliver your marketing messages—usually your marketing offers—to prospects and customers. As a result, the marketing vehicles that you use to execute your partnership marketing programs are essential to your program's success. In your company you have goals in marketing your business and solutions, which could include driving brand awareness, increasing market share and blocking competitors. Achieving your goals requires an integrated marketing approach combining your online and digital marketing with traditional programs like direct mail campaigns, call centers, event marketing and billboard advertising, along with using other media to reach your target audience and drive your business forward. It's no different when it comes to partnership marketing: Your partner brand will be leveraging your vehicles to market their product or service to your customers and audiences and/or you will be leveraging their vehicles to connect to their customers and audiences with your product or service. Here are some of the more popular partnership marketing vehicles that you can leverage in your partnership marketing program.

Online and Digital Marketing Vehicles

Websites

A website can be a primary vehicle for communicating with customers and, as a result, you may want to leverage it for communicating your offer (or leverage your offer to drive people to your website). You can use your primary website or develop a microsite, linked to the primary website, that is more catered to the program and allows for more in-depth messaging opportunities. What's more important here is to understand the metrics for the website, which include how many unique visitors and page views each section of the website receives on a monthly basis.

Permanent placement on the home pages of websites is a little more difficult to negotiate in a partner program, as that is typically where a majority of the incoming traffic lives and is considered prime real estate. If you can't give away placement or get permanent or rotating placement on your partner brands' websites, you can look into creating a pop-up, which is a form of online advertising where upon entering the website, the visitor's browser opens up a new window to promote an advertisement. More recently, websites have been using pop-unders, which are slightly different in that the advertisement is actually hidden under the active window that is already open. Pop-ups and pop-unders can be effective, yet it's important to note that these days many browsers have blocking features that allow their users to block incoming pop-ups, thereby reducing the effectiveness of the vehicle.

Websites that have e-commerce functionality provide opportunities to resell products and services. Online stores can be leveraged in your marketing partnership as well: You can promote an offer on a product, and have your partner brand resell it, take the transaction and then provide you with the information so you can ship the product to the customer. The advantage for the partner brand is that they don't have to commit to inventories and warehousing of new products and can generate revenue from sales. Websites that have a lot of stickiness—where users, visitors or customers spend a lot of time on them—are an attractive partnership marketing vehicle to a prospective partner brand, especially if the partner brand is primarily an online destination brand as opposed to a brand that primarily communicates with their customers offline.

IMDB.com (the Internet Movie Database) is one of the largest entertainment websites on the planet. They have a partnership program with Amazon.com (who owns IMDB.com) involving a permanent link on the film description web pages within IMDB.com that says, "Buy It at Amazon." A user can read about a film, decide they want to own it and click on the link to be taken to their local Amazon website where they can buy it. That's an example of IMDB leveraging the power of their website and enjoying the power of a marketing partnership with Amazon.com which goes beyond the fact that Amazon owns them.

Webinars

Webinars can be a great lead-generation vehicle, especially in B2B marketing. You can choose from a whole host of service providers like GoToMeeting or WebEx to run your webinar. Leading category experts often run webinars and many of them have quite a strong following and reach. If you have a product or service that ties well into a B2B vertical like process management, software, technology, payment systems, logistics, or warehousing and distribution, to name a few, then leveraging an endorsement from an expert and integrating your proposition into their webinar or co-sponsoring a webinar may produce some good leads for your business.

Advertising

Online advertising is what brands will typically use to market their products and services across the Web. Online advertising includes rich media, banner advertising, social network advertising, search engine marketing and link exchanges, as well as advertising on popular social networking sites. The online advertising mix for every brand is different, so be sure to get a handle on what you are doing so you can identify co-advertising opportunities for your partner.

Content

Online content comes in many forms. This could be as simple as editorial content used within a partner brand's website or as complex as the use of video or digital recordings for music, interviews and presentations. Co-developing content and e-newsletters with a partner brand presents an exciting opportunity, yet it requires a lot of planning, resources and investment. It's crucial not only to select the right partner but also to ensure that they have the capabilities that you are looking for. Many partner brands are building mobile and TV apps for products like the Apple iPhone and Vizio HDTV. Your product can be an ingredient in a popular recipe app or be featured in a gaming app. If you're going down this path, ensure that you and your partner brands have assigned obligations and responsibilities beyond the actual development of the content and that you have decided who will own it, including who will host the content, deliver it online and who will manage it.

Email Marketing and Text Messaging

A popular and cost-effective way for brands to communicate with their customers and potential customers is by using email marketing and text messaging. This includes everything from online flyers and promotional offers, to confirmation of purchase and delivery emails, to surveys, contests and questionnaires. I recently came across an email for a course on how to effectively use my BlackBerry in my business; the email was a partner offer from a major telecom network advertising a special offer to purchase a BlackBerry at a discounted price. Partner offers can be embedded in text messages (SMS) in markets where email has less usage and the penetration of cell phones is higher.

Social Media

These days most companies are turning to social networks to get their offerings in front of their audiences. If you are a B2C brand, using sites like Facebook or Twitter are effective ways to connect to your current customers and potential customers alike. It very well could be the case that your partner brand is doing a much more effective job than you are of leveraging social media platforms and has large numbers of fans, followers, friends and users. If they are open to it, you might want to think about how you can leverage their social networking pages to tap into their communities with relevant and highly targeted offers and opportunities for them, and vice versa. You also can leverage your partner brands' popular blogs and podcasts. Partnering with expert bloggers by providing content for them for use in their blogs can get your messages out to a larger audience and generate opportunities to increase visibility for your proposition.

Traditional Marketing Vehicles

TV, Radio, Print, Signage

Traditional TV, radio and print advertising as well as signage—whether a billboard or digital screen—can be leveraged as vehicles in your partnership marketing program. You can co-brand your advertising by including both partner brands to drive an offer from one to the other and share costs as a result. You see this with retailers who are driving added-value offers from manufacturers, bookstores that want to promote a title from a given author and radio campaigns that promote partner brand offers as promotions to drive traffic and customers to their websites.

Call Centers

Companies use call centers, their own or third party, to communicate with their customers and audience in many ways. Some make outbound prospecting and sales calls, others deal with customer service issues and incoming sales calls, and still others make follow-up calls to customers to get feedback on satisfaction with the service the company recently provided to them. Call centers can be leveraged in marketing partnerships as vehicles for incoming leads from a partner brand through 'warm transfer' of a customer from one call center to the other. Offers can be communicated in 'hold messages' while customers are waiting, as well as during inbound or outbound calls as an added-value promotion for purchasing a product or service on that given day or within a given time period. For some products and services, the call center is the heartbeat of the company and really is their major vehicle in driving customer acquisition; many of their marketing communications direct customers to their call center.

The costs of running a call center can be very high, which is why many companies are looking to drive their customer activities to online vehicles, but at the same time they can't abandon their call center activities altogether. This presents an opportunity for a partner brand to support and supplement the costs of running the call center with partner driven revenue in exchange for access to customers. This can prove to be quite cost-effective in comparison to launching an outbound call center of your own.

Direct Mail and Fulfillment

Direct mail is the practice of leveraging the mail or postal network in a given market to send commercial messages directly to potential or existing customers. Brands do this for several reasons, including to acquire a new customer or cross-promote another product or upgrade to an existing customer. Marketing vehicles like on-envelope, in-envelope or messaging on invoices, bills or statements present partner brands with good opportunities to reach their audience.

Most people do open up their statements when they get them in the mail or via email, making on-statement messaging an effective way to communicate an offer. The offer can be on the statement and drive the customer to a website to redeem it, it can come in the form of an insert that is placed in the envelope with the statement or it can be featured as a banner ad in the email version of the statement. Many brands send out a welcome kit in their fulfillment packs—for example, when you sign up for one of their services like hi-speed Internet for your home—and these are great places to promote partner offers as well. Other examples include awarding prizes for online contests that customers may have participated in. These are all great places to acquire a new customer, as they are much more likely to open those types of packages than the standard junk mail that they typically gets ignored.

Renewals

Another vehicle that can be leveraged to promote an offer from a partner brand is renewals. Renewals exist mostly with services that require the customer to renew at the end of a given subscription or committed period.

Whether the renewal notice is sent by email or direct mail, you can include special partner offers in the notice to communicate the value-adds that they are getting by renewing with you, further encouraging them to remain a customer. Renewals are something that customers or members will pay attention to and those envelopes or emails that go out the second or third time around to get the customer to renew may need to incentivize the end customer a little more. They could feature a compelling offer from a partner brand, especially to customers who may be thinking a little bit longer about whether they want to renew with your service.

Retail

As discussed in chapter 1, retail environments are not only physical distribution channels to resell products and to generate margin. Those same environments can be leveraged in different ways to drive partner brand offers and create awareness for products and services that don't actually go through the till (i.e., AOL CD's). This can be done by placing 'take one' slips near checkout areas of the store or by bundling them in customers' bags when they leave the store. Other opportunities can include bundling a service from a partner brand within a specific store department, for example, bundling a hi-speed Internet subscription offer with the purchase of a new laptop computer. If the store has a call center, then they can 'warm transfer' calls and create referrals to the partner brand's call center and you can leverage the retailer's websites to link to your online properties.

Products and Services

Look at your products and services and think about how you can make them better or even extend them beyond your core product into new product lines by collaborating with others. Ingredient branding can enhance your product by placing an ingredient from another brand in your existing product, like Crest Toothpaste flavored with Scope. This may generate twice the pull for your product and have you stand out against the competition. As discussed in chapter 1, licensing is a very common way to expand your brand into new product categories. Meredith Corporation has expanded their product line to make Better Homes and Gardens branded furniture available, leveraging the success that they have had with that same brand as one of their leading magazine publications. Co-marketing is another useful form of partnership marketing, where two brands get together to develop a new product and then each market the product to their respective customer bases.

Door-to-Door

Brands that market door-to-door using door drops or door hangers can place promotions from partners on their marketing collateral in exchange for a revenue stream or a contribution to the cost of producing the collateral. I've seen this with a particular chain of dry cleaners who were promoting a special offer to new customers on a door hanger from a brand that advertises residential maid services.

At-Home Service

Some brands, commonly those in the heating, air conditioning, appliance and general repair services, offer an at-home service. With contractors and technicians making visits to customers' homes, there are ample opportunities to bundle your product insert with them on a visit. This can be seen as a value-add to thank the customer for doing business with them, while it's also an opportunity for your brand to leverage the channel to gain access to homeowners. Just be sure to partner with reputable brands and those that are actually licensed to do what it is that they do and have a solid reputation on the street and online.

Contests and Lotteries

Contests and lotteries are a great way to collect customer data and can be leveraged for partnership marketing opportunities as well. You can offer a partner brand the opportunity to market to your customers on the 'customer entry forms' where they can check a box should they want to receive information from your partner brand. You may find that a fair percentage of customers may not want to, so be sure to ask if they want to receive that information. To encourage a positive response, ensure that your partner brand is relevant to the contest you are offering. Other ways of doing partnership marketing using contests and lotteries include providing a prize in exchange for promotion and publicity.

Event Marketing

An event, whether it is a half-day or a full two weeks in length, can make for a great opportunity to target an audience, especially when lots of potential target customers are getting together to share an experience. Whether it's a company-sponsored event with a keynote speaker, a major league baseball game, a premier league soccer game or the Olympics, lots of opportunity can come out of partnering with a brand that is putting on an event or with the event itself.

MBNA has it in their agreements with partners like Major League Baseball's Toronto Blue Jays that they can be on-site at the Rogers Centre for home games to sign on customers to the MBNA/Toronto Blue Jays credit card and give a sign-up gift like a free branded sports bag or T-shirt to the customers who fill out a credit card application on the spot.

Sometimes, it's not just a one-day event but a longer event like the Vancouver 2010 Olympic Winter Games, which provided brands like Omega, Birks and Acer with the opportunities to create watches, cuff links and laptop computers that were officially branded to the games. These are huge opportunities for sponsors and licensing partners alike.

Member Cards/Loyalty Program Cards

Membership cards provide opportunities for partner brands to promote special offers to customers that may have signed up for a member account with your brand. Even if there is no physical card and the account was created and generated online, by collecting the email addresses and asking for members to opt in to receive third-party communication for partner brands, you can promote special offers and discounts at different times of year to your members.

Furthermore, if you are a member of a major loyalty program, you can look into opportunities for the program to promote your offering to their entire member base from time to time as well. There may be some fees associated with it or you might have to give an exclusive offer that is better than anything on the market, but it's certainly worth considering.

Packaging (In-Pack, On-Pack, Cover-Mounts)

Manufacturers design the packaging for their products and inserts can be placed in the boxes at the manufacturers' warehouses or wherever their products are produced. There are usually fees associated with this sort of thing and the range is typically $0.01 to $0.10 per package insert, yet that is quite cost-effective when it's the only marketing cost that you have to incur. Sometimes you can get your partner brand to share in the costs, especially if you are making an exclusive and highly compelling offer available to their customers. Packaging comes in many forms, too. Offers can be placed on-pack (outside of the box) for display in retail storefronts and, in the case of print media, they can be cover-mounted on a magazine.

As per above, there are numerous ways that a brand communicates with its customers and target audience that present several points of leverage for you to explore for your partnership marketing programs. Of course, not everything you do is necessarily going to be applicable for the program that you are putting together with a given partner brand, yet it's important, whether you own your brand or work within a larger company, to gather and consider all of the information before deciding what's really available. It's easier to point out the one or two obvious marketing vehicles that jump out and scream their ability to enhance your partner program, but the risk in leaving it to those alone is that unexplored areas may provide even better opportunities. Taking the time to understand what you can truly offer your partners and what they can offer you in terms of proven and established marketing vehicles will only increase your chances for success in acquiring partners and running great partner programs after you have launched them. Be sure to leverage the vehicles that can yield the greatest results for your business.

How to Assess the Effectiveness and Value of the Marketing Vehicles

- Find out how many people walk through the partner brand's stores on a given day, visit their websites or social media pages, and read their e-newsletter and blogs. It's important that you understand the frequency of their marketing programs and how many customers they engage with on each and every one so that you can reasonably forecast results of a partnership.
- Learn what types of response rates they get for their different marketing vehicles and programs. By understanding your partner brand's marketing tactics and strategies as well as you do your own, you can leverage the most valuable vehicles to drive your program forward.
- Ask them what they do!

SOME CASE STUDIES

Meredith Corporation

Mike Burnette runs partnership marketing at Meredith Corporation, a leading American-based publisher of some of the most popular magazine titles in the country. Burnette's objective is to partner with leading brands and offer a value-add for them in the form of unique customer offers like a discounted or free magazine subscription for a year with the purchase of a partner brand's products. This is typically referred to as a 'gift with purchase,' an Added-Value Partnership as discussed in chapter 1, where Meredith is funding the offer in exchange for the opportunity to acquire new subscriptions to Meredith magazine titles. With so many titles available, Burnette has to be selective as to what partner brands to work with and what titles to match to Meredith's product offering. He has worked on marketing partnerships with brands like Edible Arrangements, FTD Florists and the AARP, to name a few. According to Burnette, "the promotional offer for the magazine title is leveraged by the partner brand as a premium value add and is used in their marketing vehicles as the brand sees fit."

The benefit for Meredith is that even though they offer their magazines at a discounted rate, or in some cases at no charge, it's a much more cost-effective way to generate subscribers for their business than by using advertising or other methods only. Furthermore, it balances out their overall cost per acquisition. In this case, the customer data that they receive upon the customer signing up for the subscription offer is worth something to Meredith, as they want to collect email addresses, work or home phone numbers, mailing addresses and other details so that they can leverage them for cross-promotional, renewal and up-selling activities at a later date.

Still, Burnette can't meet his goal if his partner brand doesn't promote the offer in their marketing vehicles. "Without the right vehicles," says Burnette, "it simply wouldn't work for us as we need to have access to partner brand websites, packaging email marketing and in-store placements to be successful." According to Burnette, "these types of partnership marketing programs now account for roughly seven-eight percent of the new subscriptions generated by Meredith on a yearly basis, which has more than doubled over the last four-year period, and furthermore, brands are now calling us directly by seeing the partnerships out there and wanting to do the same for some of their products. It's started to snowball, which has made this less of an outgoing effort for me and my team and a lot of it is now incoming." That's when you know that you've got an effective partnership marketing program in place.

crowdSPRING.com

crowdSPRING.com is an online marketplace for graphic design and copywriting. Entrepreneurs and small businesses who need designs and copy for their businesses—on everything from logos and stationery to websites and brochures—simply post what they need, when they need it and how much they want to pay. Once posted, the offer is visible to over forty-five thousand designers from one hundred and forty plus countries around the world so they can decide if they want to compete for this work. The designers submit actual designs—not bids or proposals—for the buyer to review. As the submissions come in, buyers are able to review, sort, rate, provide feedback and collaborate with designers until they find 'the one.'

Pete Burgeson, the marketing director at crowdSPRING.com, looks to leverage the power of the crowdSPRING network wherever he can. According to Burgeson, "almost all advertising is based on the premise that you need to pay someone to herd people through the doors of your business—almost all except for marketing partnerships, that is. The reason for this is that in a true marketing partnership, both parties are working together to find ways to help—instead of herding their customers. Ads are great to raise awareness and email is great to build relationships but marketing partnerships are pretty much the only cost-effective way for us to reach new and discrete communities of customers and to gain a trusted referral from another business that members of those communities already trust." Burgeson continues to explain that "leveraging existing and already developed marketing vehicles, whether they are online or offline, from a partner brand can provide access to discrete audiences that you would never be able to affordably target on your own as a small or mid-sized company."

Companies like crowdSPRING understand that their customers, websites, email addresses and their 'crowdsourcing' community are valuable assets and can provide highly targeted access to creatives and small and medium-sized business owners for the right partner brand. That is powerful stuff and if leveraged properly, they pose some great opportunities to partner with other brands who will make compelling vehicles available in return.

Cocktail Marketing

According to Chris Reed, the former managing director at Cocktail Marketing in London, U.K., his partnership marketing philosophy of how to leverage marketing vehicles is pretty simple.

"We're a dating agency for brands. We put synergistic brands together. We do this by looking at where brands are and where they want to go; who their customers are and the brand DNA and then we match this analysis with potential brand partners. We know, because of our experience and constant contacts, what these possible brand partners are looking for and whether they welcome brand partnerships at all. We then negotiate with several brand partners and create the best possible partnership solution for our client brand."

"We use instinct and experience more than hard research as often research tells you where a brand is, not where it wants to be and brand partnerships are all about positive future brand association. We meet with brands and discuss and then we match them with brands that will help them to achieve their marketing and sales objectives."

"We believe that brand partnerships can achieve any marketing objective from loyalty to brand awareness, website traffic driving to footfall driving, and media to sales."

Reed cites a partnership marketing case study for a marketing partnership that he worked on with Waterstones (a leading bookseller) and Thomson (a leading package holiday provider) in the U.K. and how they leveraged several marketing vehicles to put it into play:

> "Thomson, the U.K.'s largest travel agent, and Waterstones, the U.K.'s largest book retailer, were the perfect partners when themed around travel. Waterstones gained a partnership with a recognizable and trusted brand in their stores, which would encourage increased spending and bring people in store, and they also gained a promotion in Thomson stores driving footfall from one retailer to another. Thomson gained the same. Therefore both brands gained two partnership promotions. Neither brand paid for the other's incentives nor did each pay for each other's marketing literature. All quid pro quo."

Waterstones' customers receive £100 off their next Thomson holiday when they pick up a leaflet in store. The program was supported in Waterstones stores with

- Posters
- Shelf talkers
- Table edges
- Table headers
- Leaflet dispensers

- Shelf headers
- Window decals

Thomsons' booking customers received a booklet offering over £50 worth of discounts at Waterstones. The program was supported by Thomson with

- Posters
- Email newsletter placement
- Online placement on websites

According to Reed, "The partnership marketing campaign was considered a great success for both parties, driving footfall to storefronts as well as sales/bookings, and the media value of the exposure that was given to both parties exceeded £350,000, which is something unheard of as brands can't typically buy that space or don't have the budgets to do so, and through the partnership, they did not have to and were able to reach new customers in untapped communications channels."

Another case study that Reed likes to refer to is that of the Fitness First Member Rewards program they facilitated in years past. Fitness First is an international chain of health clubs operating worldwide in over fifteen countries, yet this program was specific to their U.K. operations.

"The Fitness First Club is a classic loyalty club where it's all about the strength of the brand partners and how they relate to the lifestyles and aspirations of the Fitness First customers and how they reflect positively on the Fitness First brand itself. Fitness First in turn gives brand endorsement and brand exposure to the partner brands in return for the partner brands endorsing Fitness First and giving them an incentive in return. Everyone wins."

The objective for Chris and his team on this project was to source eight marketing partners to join in the launch of 'First Club' by Fitness First—a member benefits program offering discounts and rewards for all Fitness First members. The marketing partners would commit to a one-year term with offers that could rotate on a monthly or quarterly basis. The program was developed and designed to run as a rewards program for existing Fitness First members.

Fitness First was offering their marketing Partners this in return:

- Presence on the Fitness First website
- Presence on the First Club microsite
- A unique landing page
- Presence on emails to members
- Point of Sale materials
- Fitness First Network TV advertising in clubs

As a result, Chris and his team successfully created partnerships with the following brands:

- Hertz
- ASOS
- RAC
- La Senza
- Superdrug
- Waterstones
- ATOC
- Best Western Hotels

According to Reed, "Fitness First was able to offer all First Club members compelling discounts from the aforementioned partner brands, which were carefully selected as ones that would be relevant to the target audience. Fitness First was able to offer this as a true value-add to their customers and benefit from positive brand association as well. The partner brands were able to target their desired audience directly. No conflicting brands in the mix meant increased cut-through for each of the partner brands and each benefited from long-term brand association with a premium brand like Fitness First, which elevated their profile."

. . .

If marketing is the strategic process by which we sell goods and services to meet the needs and wants of our customers, then partnership marketing is the strategic process by which we leverage marketing vehicles to help partner brands meet their sales and marketing goals and objectives. Know your marketing vehicles and ask your prospective partner brand for a list of their marketing vehicles as well. Use win-win-win marketing vehicles in your marketing partnerships to increase your chances of success. Use the best ones for you, your partner and the customer to make it easy for the latter to redeem offers and enjoy a highly compelling customer experience.

Dan Morton, director of partnership marketing at Reliant Energy, has worked in partner marketing for the majority of his career, holding various roles with Microsoft, AOL, Vonage and now Reliant Energy. He often has emphasized the importance of partner accountability when speaking about partnership marketing, but more importantly, the need for them (the partner brand) to have 'the goods in place' to be successful. According to Morton, "a marketing partnership and the success of it is highly dependent on the partners' placement of the partner brand's proposition in their marketing vehicles and ensuring that they leverage the right ones and commit to doing so." Morton goes on to emphasize that "the partner brand needs to be rewarded and see incentive to make key placements available in their marketing vehicles; without that incentive, it's likely not going to happen."

That incentive can come in the form of a unique product, highly compelling offer or the opportunity to generate significant revenue for their business, which I refer to as the partner value proposition (which we will discuss in chapter 7). Morton says that "the most difficult part of developing marketing partnerships is that many companies and industries are unfamiliar with it all. They struggle to see the potential return and get very caught up in what they will have to give up to the other partner in order to effectively execute the program . . . without much experience in running partnership marketing activities, it can be a little scary even though in the true sense, it's very much a low risk alternative to what they are already doing to grow their business."

●   ●   ●

Leveraging a partner brand's assets like their brand, customers and marketing vehicles often requires a 'proof of concept' and transparency as well as some detailed information on what the partnership will do for them. How will it help their business and what benefits will it provide? Now that you understand the importance of leveraging partnership marketing assets, in the next chapter we will discuss how you can leverage them to grow your business.

3

Using Partnership Marketing to Generate Revenue and Decrease Costs

MARKETING PARTNERSHIPS THAT USE the principles and practices of smart collaboration can help a brand, whether it is a company, association, non-profit or community organization, achieve their revenue growth objectives. Such partnerships have a direct link to driving revenue for the brand, with one of the many advantages being that the performance metrics, if properly established, can be measured easily. Partnership marketing can be the strategy that you use to increase revenue in your business in the following three ways, which will be discussed throughout this chapter:

1. New customer acquisition
2. Increasing average transactional value from customers
3. Increasing average number of transactions from customers

NEW CUSTOMER ACQUISITION

Partnership marketing programs can enhance customer acquisition activities and become a bigger part of the marketing channel mix in an effort to reduce costs and expenditure and optimize the profitability of your business. Your strategy to acquire more customers may include partnership marketing as a part of your overall marketing strategy or partnership marketing might be your main strategy for customer acquisition. Examples that demonstrate how different types of businesses make partnership marketing a part of their strategy to acquire customers are discussed later in this chapter.

There are lots of ways (acquisition channels) to acquire new customers for your brand. To name a few, you can buy a customer list and cold-call them, advertise in a popular trade magazine offline, use Google Adwords online, do direct marketing (online or offline) and have referral arrangements with suppliers. You can leverage the power of online social networks and email marketing, and assemble an outbound 'inside sales team'. All are effective strategies, and having a well-rounded mix of acquisition channels that you are testing and optimizing is a common approach in business today.

Cost per Acquisition (CPA)

One of the biggest issues that marketers face is how to lower the cost of acquiring a new customer. Every business faces this challenge. Why? Because they all need to acquire new customers to increase their revenue. Some of the more common marketing channels that brands have used in the past are becoming much more costly to implement and the success of the campaigns is no longer there.

Mass advertising, direct marketing campaigns and programs targeted to the public at large are generally less cost-effective. Such strategies are usually more effective when used for launching a product in a new product category, as the market for it is in the infancy stage of the product life cycle and the focus is on creating brand awareness. However, as time passes and the product is subject to more direct and indirect competition, the opportunity to acquire those customers through such methods decreases and becomes more costly. The reality is that with increased competition in a given space, it can cost as much as three to four times what it would have a few years earlier when you first launched the product category. As a result, a shift toward more cost-effective marketing channels is crucial to ensure sustainable profitability for the business.

The optimal acquisition strategy is to find an approach that meets your customer acquisition targets while keeping your overall CPA as low as possible. It is important to factor in CPA when determining the optimal mix of acquisition channels. Setting up a measurable strategy enables you to properly track CPA and measure the results of your acquisition programs.

Of course, there are differences in the approach and therefore costs incurred to acquire a new customer, as every product and business is unique. The travel industry is not the same as the consumer packaged-goods industry or the computer industry, and therefore the factors that go into determining the CPA will be specific to each industry. Still, for all categories, as current marketing spending becomes less and less effective at acquiring a new customer, the business needs alternative channels to offset the increasing costs that they face for customer acquisition–related programs. A channel shift is needed to bring overall costs down.

The answer is not necessarily to just abandon your core marketing activities altogether, as they have been your bread and butter for so long, but, to improve profit margins, perhaps you enhance them with partnership marketing programs that are typically more cost-effective (because in most cases, the partner brand is responsible for the marketing expenses). Products go through life cycles and once a market for a given product has been heavily penetrated, that product has less and less of a pool of potential new customers to draw from. At that point, customer acquisition activities have to be more targeted as it's not about drawing in the mass volume that you once did, but drawing them in at the cost that you once did.

Let's look at an example of a value-added partnership marketing program, specifically at the expected costs associated with the program and the forecasted CPA that will result, depending on the response rate, for a given brand. In this example, a given long distance phone service company (PSC) has decided to partner with an original equipment manufacturer (OEM) of digital home phones. The agreement is that the PSC will provide a special offer of one free month of long distance in North America on their North American long distance phone service to customers who purchase the OEM's latest digital home phone pack. The offer is to be promoted on-pack with a sticker and in-pack with a leaflet, both driving the customer to the PSC's website to register and take up the special offer. The PSC has calculated that their costs to run the program are $100,000 for marketing collateral, $1,000 for shipping the collateral to the OEM's warehouse and $2,000 for designing the promotional web page that will feature the offer and allow the new customers to register for their service, for a total cost of $103,000. The special offer is to be bundled with 250,000 units of the OEM's latest digital home phone pack. The CPA projection scenarios are outlined on the following page.

In terms of the recent marketing strategies of the PSC, they ran a direct mail campaign with a well-segmented list of potential customers that resulted in a CPA of $125, along with their call center operation of cold-calling leads, which resulted in a CPA of $175. Their current focus is to create a new campaign that meets the desired customer acquisition targets while reducing the overall cost of acquiring new customers, and are therefore interested in exploring the world of partnership marketing, which is a new strategy for them. With the knowledge in hand that they typically get a 0.60% response rate on their direct mail campaigns, they figure that using 0.50%, 0.75% and 1.00% as guidelines for scenarios would be more than realistic to calculate their projected CPA for the program. They plug the numbers in to their spreadsheet and forecast that their CPA will range from as high as $82.40 to as low as $41.20 and are excited about the prospect of reducing their overall CPA.

If you are properly tracking your customer acquisition marketing activities and programs, you can easily track the value that such a partnership can bring. The PSC has an opportunity to bundle their proposition with a leading OEM that also targets the same types of customers and operates within the same vertical category (telecommunications). The propensity for someone to want to make a switch or try a new long distance phone service dramatically increases when that individual moves to a new dwelling, has a change in behavior in their existing dwelling or receives a compelling opportunity to change. The purchase of a new digital home phone unit could mean that they are moving or growing their family and phone users at home, could

		Partnership Program—CPA Projections		
Item	**Cost**			
Marketing Collateral	$100,000			
Shipping of Collateral	$1,000			
Promotional Web Page Design	$2,000			
	$103,000			
Scenario 1	**Units**	**Response Rate 1**	**New Customers Acquired**	**Customer Acquisition Cost**
	250,000	1%	2,500	$41.20
Scenario 2	**Units**	**Response Rate 2**	**New Customers Acquired**	**Customer Acquisition Cost**
	250,000	0.75%	1,875	$54.93
Scenario 3	**Units**	**Response Rate 3**	**New Customers Acquired**	**Customer Acquisition Cost**
	250,000	0.50%	1,250	$82.40

it not? It could also mean that their current phone is no longer working and it's time to get a new one. The point is that the customer is thinking about their phone and how they use it and want to use it going forward, so it's a great opportunity to capture that thinking with a special offer on long distance phone service.

Why does this partnership work? The benefit to the PSC is that they can target customers with a relevant phone service offering on the spot when they purchase a digital home phone unit, giving them instant access to a unique and highly compelling offer. In addition, they can acquire those new customers more cost effectively than they are currently acquiring them via their direct mail programs and outbound call center operation, because the offer is targeted to customers thinking about phones and likely related phone services. The benefit to the OEM is that they have a solid added-value offering to enhance their proposition and make them unique in a highly competitive 'phone set' market because they are offering something that nobody else has, given that the PSC is working with them exclusively as their national OEM partner.

As in the case above, partnership marketing can help you meet your customer acquisition objectives at lower costs and, as a result, compensate for more costly marketing channels, reducing your overall cost per new customer acquired.

How to Track a Partnership Marketing Program

Creating a partnership marketing program with key metrics in order to be able to measure the success of the program is a fundamental component to the overall initiative. The foundation of most partnership marketing activities is that they are measurable, allowing each customer acquired to be tracked back to the related campaign that brought in that customer.

There are a number of ways that measurement of a campaign can be accomplished. Tracking of a program is typically done by assigning a 'unique identifier' to a given partner company, whereby every time a new customer or member or client is acquired via a marketing campaign or program, the customer is linked to that partner company and can be fully traced back to them. E-commerce-based businesses especially are taking advantage of opportunities where promotion codes or account numbers are pre-populated in the online registration processes or the checkout pages that customers complete. In the above example, the PSC had a unique identifier on the in-pack leaflet, which was then used when registering on the PSC's website to activate the one month of free long distance. Therefore, every customer that goes to the PSC's website to take advantage of the special offer will complete the process on a web page where the unique program identifier is entered, thereby letting the PSC know that the customer came from their OEM partner, which makes for a measurable program with their partner.

How to Achieve Customer Growth While Reducing CPA

Your marketing channel mix may need to change over time as your products move to different stages in the product life cycle. Let's say you start with a marketing budget of $1 million, which is to be used to acquire new customers—with a target of acquiring ten thousand customers. The mix that is keeping you on target with that budget could very well look like this:

YEAR 1					
Channel	Total Budget	% of Budget	New Customers	% of Customers	CPA
Call Center	$350,000	35	2,000	20	$175
Offline Advertising	$150,000	15	1,100	11	$136
Online Advertising	$50,000	5	650	6.5	$77
Direct Mail	$200,000	20	1,600	16	$125
Email Marketing	$50,000	5	1,000	10	$50
Social Media	$10,000	1	200	2	$50
Partnership Marketing	$190,000	19	3,450	34.5	$55
Total	$1,000,000	100%	10,000	100%	$100

Now, what would happen if next year, you have been told that the target CPA for the company is $85 instead of $100? The economy is slowing down and every department has been hit with a budget cut, including yours. While the expectation is that there will not be any customer growth next year, the target for new customer acquisitions still remains at 10,000. Therefore, a target of 10,000 new customers and a target CPA of $85 will give you a revised marketing budget of $850,000. It appears clear, very quickly, that the only way to achieve these targets is to change your marketing mix. It is true that the call center and advertising efforts might have generated significant customer acquisitions in the past; however, the cost to acquire these customers is too high and you cannot afford such rich programs, based on your revised marketing budget. Where do you begin?

A great place to start is focusing on current marketing initiatives with lower CPA. You will need to conduct a detailed analysis of each marketing channel in order to evaluate the maximum potential you can achieve from a program and the maximum opportunity there is to acquire customers within each channel. For example, while email marketing, with a low CPA, was only five percent of your budget and generated ten percent of your customer base, you must evaluate how many incremental customers you can acquire if you increase your marketing budget for this channel. You cannot do this through simple math but rather you must evaluate what programs would be available through this channel and if they would achieve your objective of increased customers.

For the purpose of this example, the aforementioned analysis was performed and the following marketing channel mix was developed to meet your CPA target of $85:

YEAR 2					
Channel	Total Budget	% of Budget	New Customers	% of Customers	CPA
Call Center	$150,000	18	850	8.5	$176
Offline Advertising	$0	0	0	0	$0
Online Advertising	$150,000	18	1,875	18.75	$80
Direct Mail	$200,000	23	1,600	16	$125
Email Marketing	$0	0	0	0	$0
Social Media	$0	0	0	0	$0
Partnership Marketing	$350,000	41	5,675	56.75	$62
Total	$850,000	100%	10,000	100%	$85

Partnership marketing is not the only kind of marketing that marketers can leverage to acquire new customers for their business. It is merely one type or channel of marketing and in many cases a mix of many marketing channels is necessary to drive the business forward and specifically to increase revenue. One thing for sure, though, smart marketing partnerships that leverage the assets, budgets and resources of both companies can certainly reduce the overall cost of customer acquisition for a given company.

Some Case Studies

As discussed in this chapter, a company can use partnership marketing as a small part of their marketing strategy, as the core of their marketing strategy or as something in between. The reality is that if you take a closer look at your favorite brands and what they are up to, you will see that for many of them, partnership marketing is at the core of their customer acquisition strategy.

Let's look at a few business examples and how they incorporate partnership marketing into their customer acquisition strategy.

Microsoft

Could Microsoft have become who they are today without a successful marketing partnership with IBM back in 1980 to adapt and develop the operating system for the IBM personal computer? Sure, today, the PC (Personal Computer) equipped with the Microsoft OS (Operating System) is the industry standard, yet, looking back, what got Microsoft there? I've never met Bill Gates or anyone else who was around in the early days of Microsoft, but I am going to go out on a limb and say that without having had that opportunity to develop the aforementioned operating system known (back in the day) as MS-DOS, Microsoft likely would not be as big a brand as they are today. Gates partnered with IBM but did not transfer the copyright of the operating system to IBM, because he believed that other hardware vendors would clone IBM's computers, creating more opportunities with other OEMs in the market for his product. That is exactly what happened. Gates then was able to partner with all of the other OEMs like Hewlett-Packard and Compaq, for example, and sell the MS-DOS system outside of IBM to generate even more revenue for Microsoft. Today, pretty much every PC is bundled with the modern-day version and latest release of the Microsoft OS. If you were to buy a Dell computer tomorrow, it would be delivered to you bundled with 'Microsoft Windows 7.'

MBNA (Bank of America)

Take a company like MBNA, who in recent years was acquired by Bank of America in a move to take a leading share of the affinity credit card market. Most people have never heard of MBNA and are much more familiar with product brand names like VISA, MasterCard, American Express and Discover Card, to name a few in the credit card space. Still, MBNA is not a small operation. Although they are not a 'destination brand' or a brand that consumers will know off the top of their heads, they are leaders in the affinity credit card market and have built their business through years and years of partnering with other brands to power their credit card offering. How does it work? MBNA enters into a three-way marketing partnership with MasterCard and any one of their partner brands in the pro sports, auto, education, travel and hospitality verticals. MBNA has developed hundreds if not thousands of marketing partnerships over the years in the U.S., Canada, U.K. and other countries. With partner brands like Major League Baseball's New York Yankees, MBNA (now branded Bank of America) gives fans of the famous baseball team who sign up for the no-fee Yankees credit card an opportunity to obtain special offers on merchandise, memorabilia and other unique experiences. MBNA brings the full turnkey solution, along with their partnership with MasterCard, to a potential partner brand, offering this credit card as an added value to the partner brand's customers, in exchange for access to their customers through various customer communication vehicles like the Yankees websites, home games and direct mail campaigns. It's a powerful relationship that drives revenue for both parties and helps to explain why traditional banks offering credit cards have recently jumped into doing affinity credit card partnerships of their own in an effort to claim their fair share of the available market. For MBNA, their main strategy for acquiring customers is through partnership marketing initiatives. Without their partner brands, who provide MBNA with access to their customers, MBNA would not have a means to generate revenue for their business.

Demand Metric

Jesse Hopps, CEO of Demand Metric, a business services company, was looking to change his marketing channel mix and focus more on leveraging marketing partnerships to drive brand awareness and generate revenue from his target audience—small and mid-sized businesses. Hopps' brand value proposition is a subscription-based offering to leaders of businesses (presidents, CEOs, owners) who, after signing up and paying the monthly fee, gain access to more than three hundred practical, tried and tested sales and marketing tools and templates. Hopps realizes that there are opportunities outside of the subscription model. As well as this model has worked for him to date, there are some potential customers that will have more specific needs and therefore require a more targeted solution. Hopps' plan is to leverage marketing partners who have a link to his target audience in an effort to make unique 'product bundles' available for specific subjects like project management, sales, branding and social media, to name a few. The marketing partners could then resell these products to their customers and members and facilitate the distribution that Hopps is looking for. By taking on a partnership marketing strategy, Hopps can effectively continue to market his subscription-based product directly and market new product bundles as a one-time sale via his marketing partners. Such a strategy would result in incremental sales and revenue for Demand Metric beyond their core product offering.

I have had the opportunity to work with Demand Metric, who have now partnered with leading associations like San Diego–based Vistage to offer unique toolkits at compelling prices for Vistage members, who are made up of over fifteen thousand CEOs worldwide. According to Hopps, the strategy is to present additional offerings in the marketplace and to create bespoke options for marketing partners like Vistage who may require something unique and different for their member base. Demand Metric's marketing partnership with Vistage provides them with access to a large potential customer base and the opportunity to target these members with a proposition that makes sense. Vistage benefits by having a strong content offering for their members and by gaining incremental revenue from sales of the Demand Metric toolkits.

Fender

Del Breckenfeld, author of *The Cool Factor: How to build your brand's image through Partnership Marketing* (Wiley, October 2008) and director of entertainment marketing at Fender comments on how Fender was able to enter into a successful marketing partnership with Harmonix, with a focus on creating access to new customers.

According to Breckenfeld, ever since video games became a dominant seller among pre-teens, teens and young adults, music instrument manufacturers, guitar makers in particular, began to question how they could ever compete against such a phenomenon. If you compared the price of an entry-level guitar with a video game deck, they were pretty close. As the holiday season approached, this was especially challenging for the guitar companies because that fourth quarter traditionally accounted for approximately forty percent of their annual sales. When it came to a Christmas wish list for pre-teens and teens, guitars ran a distant second, if they were on the list at all, to video game systems.

Breckenfeld shares the story of when he received an invitation to a top-secret meeting at Fender headquarters in Scottsdale, Arizona, with the executives of Harmonix, the company that originally developed Guitar Hero. Harmonix was launching a new and improved version of Guitar Hero called Rock Band, and they wanted the Fender brand to add credibility to this new venture. The original Guitar Hero had been supported by Gibson, a competitor to Fender, which had the plastic Guitar Hero controllers modeled after their guitars. With four Fender representatives in attendance at that meeting, under the strictest non-disclosure agreement, it was clear to Fender that this offer was a once-in-a-lifetime opportunity for the Fender brand to reach a new audience (gamers) through one of the hottest new video game platforms. The new game was also to feature a full band: in addition to guitar and bass, you would also have a drum kit, hence the name Rock Band. Furthermore, Harmonix wanted the guitar and bass controllers to be authentic replicas (still in plastic), not just look-alikes as they were with the original Guitar Hero controllers. This was very exciting to Fender because it would give the gamer the feel of what it was like to play an actual Fender guitar. Fender hoped that such an experience would encourage the gamer to want to invest in and learn how to play a real Fender guitar.

According to the National Association of Music Merchants, guitar sales in 2007 were relatively flat as compared to previous years. Fender associated a lot of value with the partnership with Harmonix to meet customer acquisition targets. Rock Band was released in December 2007 and has sold approximately four million units, with over thirty million songs downloaded to date.

For Fender, Offworld research (posted by Brandon Boyd, November 25, 2008) showed that sixty-seven percent of people who played the game said they were at least interested in picking up an instrument, and Fender's largest retail chain, Guitar Center, showed a twenty-seven percent jump in sales to first-time buyers after Rock Band launched. According to *Times Online* (December 1, 2008), a report conducted by Youth Music found that of the twelve million young people aged three to eighteen in the United States, more than half played music video games. A fifth of those gamers said that they "now played an instrument after catching the musical bug from the games." Timed with the 2009 updated version of Rock Band, for the first time, Fender offered guitar controllers made of wood (distributed by Mad Catz) outfitted with the Rock Band game electronics to bring potential consumers one step closer to the experience of actually playing a real musical instrument.

For the Fender brand, Rock Band was the perfect partnership platform to target a new audience (gamers) by combining resources at a fraction of the cost it would have otherwise paid to reach them. The strategic placement of the Fender brand for the video game Rock Band and the replicas of their famous Stratocaster guitars taking shape in the form of these video game guitar controllers is without question a profitable partnership for Fender. Licensing rights and revenues aside, the ability to get one of their products in the hands of those interested in rock music, even from just the gaming side of it, could very well lead to them selling more and more real Fender guitars and capturing the market share for a whole new generation of guitar players. For Rock

Band, the Fender brand gives more authenticity to the look and feel of their instruments and allows their customers to enjoy the experience even more.

INCREASING AVERAGE TRANSACTIONAL VALUE (ATV) FROM CUSTOMERS

Business growth is largely dependent on what your customers are willing to spend on your products or services and what volume they are willing to buy. One of the ways that a business can generate more revenue is to increase the ATV for each customer. This can be achieved through several methods.

Beauty salons are quite effective at increasing the ATV per visit. Typically, their customers will come in for a spa treatment or a haircut, which is their core product offering and value proposition. You will often see at a beauty salon that they offer some type of shampoo or conditioner at a special offer price in conjunction with one of their partner brands. They then sell that product for $20 to the customer and have increased the ATV per visit, as a result.

Companies like GoDaddy.com do this when they sell you a URL for your new online business. On the checkout page, once you have confirmed the URL you are purchasing, they offer a whole suite of partner services from web design to Internet security and hosting. URLs are the core offering from GoDaddy.com, yet over the years they have partnered with several companies to offer their customers more services and thereby increase the ATV per visit.

Another way to increase ATV is to package together a set of complementary products or services. By creating higher perceived value from the new product that you have created with your partner brand, you can now charge more for the product. People are willing to pay more if they think they are getting more. In chapter 1, I discussed the example of the Tymekeeper, where Pearl Drums was including this value-added product with the purchase of certain types of drum kits. As a market leader, Pearl does not want to reduce the price of their drums; they want people to pay for the premium brand and product that they have built their reputation on. As a result, packaging the Tymekeeper with their drum sets and marketing that the Tymekeeper has a retail value of $150 allows Pearl to increase the prices of their drums without negatively affecting their sales. Customers feel as though they are getting something exclusive with the Pearl drum kit—something that they are not able to purchase anywhere else.

INCREASING THE AVERAGE NUMBER OF TRANSACTIONS (ANT) FROM CUSTOMERS

Another way to grow your business is by increasing the ANT that your customers make with you. It is necessary to give customers more products and services to choose from if you want to increase the ANT from customers, and partnership marketing can help you to offer those additional products and services. This is especially helpful if your offering is made up of only one product or service.

In chapter 1, I discussed added-value marketing partnerships, and gave the example of Bell and Starbucks. This partnership had the ability to achieve a number of business objectives, one of them being to increase the ANT from customers. While most customers might just walk into Starbucks, pick up a coffee and leave, by encouraging customers to stay in the coffee shop for longer by making the added-value offer of free wireless Internet through Bell, Starbucks increases the chances that their customers make more than one transaction with them during their visit. They might purchase a second cup of coffee, a sandwich as lunchtime approaches or an afternoon snack. With the free Internet service that customers are now getting access to, they could easily make one or two more additional transactions over the course of time that they are in the store.

Amazon.com has a program called Seller Central, which allows e-commerce Web partners who want to sell their products and services on Amazon.com the ability to do so without Amazon.com having to carry inventory, merchandise their product online and ship orders to customers. This distribution type of marketing partnership program has allowed thousands of approved Amazon.com merchant partners to leverage Amazon.com traffic to drive sales of their products within the Amazon universe. According to the Amazon.com website, "Seller Central is the Web interface used to manage all aspects of selling on Amazon. You can add product information, make inventory updates, manage orders, and manage payments through a suite of Web-based and downloadable tools." The benefit to the seller is that they gain access to the customers of one of the largest online retailers on the planet. The benefit to Amazon.com is that they are now able to offer their customers more products and a wider selection of product categories without having to incur the costs of warehousing inventories, and they generate revenue by earning a commission on every product sale. Amazon.com handles the transaction for their Seller Central Merchant Partners, keeps their commission and deposits the balance in their partners' bank accounts. It's all very seamless. Upon receiving a customer order, Amazon.com communicates with the partner and provides them with the order details and information, and the Seller Central Merchant Partner takes over in fulfilling the order and shipping it to the end customer. This arrangement results in Amazon.com's customers making more transactions with the site, as they will visit more often, knowing that Amazon.com is constantly adding more products. As a result, customers may spend less time on other shopping websites and increase the ANT on the Amazon.com site.

You may find that you don't want to sell other products, but want to sell to your customers more of the same product over and over again several times a week, month or year. Say that you own a chain of sandwich shops and want to sell more sandwiches to your existing customers. You need to come up with something to incentivize them to visit you more and increase the average number of transactions or store visits they make with you. You come across a loyalty card program run by a pizza restaurant down the street. Basically, it is buy ten slices of pizza and get the next one free; the owners of the restaurant stamp your card every time you purchase a slice of pizza. You like it, but the idea of giving away free sandwiches is not sitting well with you. You see your sandwiches as a premium product and you are not interested in discounting the price or giving the sandwiches away for free, and incurring the costs to do so. After all, you have to print up the cards and distribute them and there are costs associated with that as it is. Then you say to yourself, why do I need to give my own sandwiches away? Why don't I find a partner brand like a local Blu-ray, DVD and video game rental retailer who can offer a free game or video rental to my customers when they buy ten sandwiches? The partner brand would benefit from the advertising and exposure that I would be giving to them, as well as from the potential to acquire new customers that come in for their free rental. It's cost-effective and they can restrict the offer to only certain movie or game titles to ensure that they are not giving away their premium titles. This could only be a win-win. You print up the cards, the partner brand funds the free offer (as they benefit from the new channel of customers) and you have a loyalty program that doesn't eat into your costs beyond the design and printing of the loyalty cards, all while achieving your strategy of increasing the ANT per customer.

•   •   •

Marketing partnerships help acquire customers, increase your average transactional value from existing customers and increase the number of transactions your customers make with you, all the while being more cost effective than if you were to do it alone. Still, it will only work for you if you can prove that the marketing partnerships that you are considering are economically valuable not only for yourself but also for your partner brands. Our next chapter discusses the importance of being economically connected as partners and why that is a necessary component of your success over the life of your partnership marketing programs.

4

ECP: Economic Connection as Partners

A PERSONAL RELATIONSHIP IS a relationship that has 'an emotional connection between people.' Think of your friends. You probably would not refer to them as friends if you were not connected to them emotionally and therefore drawn to them as people. Think of personal relationships in the context of your family. You don't choose them, but you are emotionally connected to them, unless you choose not to be.

When personal relationships are going well, it's typically because the connection is strong and the parties involved are receiving significant value from them. They are highly engaged in each other's lives as a result. When it's not going so well, it's usually because at least one of the parties is no longer receiving what they need from the relationship and the connection starts to weaken or dissolve altogether.

Why am I speaking about personal relationships in a book on partnership marketing? As much as the variables are different for a marketing partnership versus that of a personal relationship, the basic principles are quite similar. Ask yourself the question: What connects marketing partners? The economic value that they are both receiving from each other. Without that highly important economic value, there is virtually no reason to be in a marketing partnership that requires a commitment of time, energy and resources. If personal relationships have 'an emotional connection between people,' then I propose that a marketing partnership could very well be defined as 'an economic connection between partners.'

Think about it for a moment: Marketing partnerships are meant to help achieve the sales and marketing goals of the partner brands by launching a series of key initiatives in the marketplace—whether they are longer-term strategic programs that provide ongoing results or a series of shorter-term tactical partner promotions that meet more immediate goals. It's all about the economic value generated from the marketing partnership, and if that value is significant, then the relationship likely reflects it. Without that highly coveted economic value, the marketing partnership is destined to struggle for relevancy to the partner brands and likely will be ignored by both and fizzle out over time.

The most rewarding marketing partnerships will do more for the partner brands than you ever thought possible (like the most rewarding personal relationships do for people). They will help the partner brands acquire new customers, strengthen and supplement their unique brands and keep their existing customers loyal for longer. Such marketing partnerships exhibit what I like to call 'a strong economic connection as partners' (ECP):

Personal Relationships	Marketing Partnerships
Emotional	Economic
Connection	Connection
People	Partners

Ultimately, marketing partnerships with a strong ECP will be more than on the company radar. Most employees are not only aware of them, but understand the value they bring to the organization. They understand that these marketing partnerships encompass a broad range of initiatives, and that these partnerships demonstrate the true essence of brand collaboration—sharing of budgets, customers, communications vehicles and sales channels. They understand how other marketing programs are leveraging and gaining from incorporating partnership marketing initiatives into all areas of the marketing channel mix, and that this approach can enhance, support and supplement what they are already doing.

Let's look into more detail about what creating a strong ECP really means.

ECONOMIC

Can we help each other? Can we drive value for each other economically? The first part of ECP is the 'E,' which does not stand for 'emotional' as in the case of a personal relationship. In a marketing partnership, the emotional component of ECP is replaced by 'economic,' which is what drives a successful business relationship. The partner brands are typically getting together for one underlying reason: to drive economic value from the relationship. Marketing partnerships that are built on, and are developed as a result of, an emotional connection without a sound opportunity to drive that all-important economic value back to all participating partner brands are not only faulty by nature, they steer resources and working capital away from opportunities that will drive economic value. For example, perhaps your company CEO likes tennis and therefore gets behind a sponsorship partnership with a national tennis event for the two weeks that it's in town. He has the authority to lock up that deal, but is it the best deal for the company? Is it worth the marketing cost that will be incurred in comparison to participating in other marketing partnerships that might generate even more new customers or transactions from existing customers? It might very well be a good fit, if your company sells tennis balls, sports clothing or something else that is linked to the tennis event. But, is a liking for the sport of tennis alone a good business reason for creating a marketing partnership?

We are all familiar with the saying that it's not 'what you know, but who you know.' In the business world, that definitely holds some truth, but in the partnership marketing world, should the criteria for making partnership decisions be based on who you know? Should a decision to partner with another company be based on the fact that you are 'good friends' with the marketing director at another company? Should 'emotion' and 'ease of facilitation' be the only factors that carry weight when it comes to which companies you should be partnering with? In a word, no. Creating a marketing partnership just for the sake of having one is not necessarily going to help you achieve the economic value you are looking for from your partner brand. It is all about affiliating with a brand that has the potential and willingness to drive economic value from the marketing partnership.

Determining an acceptable level of economic value is really up to you. A given brand's key success metrics could very well be different from another brand and it's influenced by what your business is about, what stage of the business life cycle your business is in and how you are looking to grow in the coming years. There are many ways to grow your business, and while this is not a book on strategic growth priorities per se, for the sake of this conversation, the following three priorities are the ones that I have come across most often over the course of my career:

Increase Revenue/Market Share Through an Increase in Customers

A classic example of this is leveraging a distribution marketing partnership to market your products to the partner brands customers and acquire those customers as your own. If successful, you are earning revenue from new customers (or at least the potential to earn revenue) where you did not do so before.

Increase Mind Share Through Brand Awareness

Marketing partnerships can drive economic value in different forms. In the case of sponsorship programs or content marketing, you are leveraging the reach that a given partner brand has with your target audience and are making your brand highly visible to them, driving awareness for your brand, products, services, websites, etc. as a result.

Increase Profitability Through Lower Customer Acquisition Costs

It costs money, time and resources to market on your own. Everyone needs to do it, but if you are looking to bring costs down, then aligning yourself with a marketing partner who can deliver your offer to their customers will bring down the overall customer acquisition cost for your business and balance out those costly direct marketing and media channels. Added-value marketing partnerships may commit you to giving a unique offer or even a free trial of your product or service to the customers of your partner brand, but it's a cost that most companies are willing to incur for not having to spend dollars on marketing materials, collateral and other marketing activities when marketing directly.

All of the above—increasing revenue/market share, increasing mind share and increasing profitability—are reliable indicators for growth in any organization. If your company has been able to achieve all three, then you're likely sitting in a pretty good place right about now. If you have not achieved any of them, then you have some work to do. For the sake of this discussion, let's assume that those are the strategic growth priorities for your organization and that pretty much every initiative that everyone in the organization is working on must contribute to them. Consider the following:

- What about your marketing partnerships; what contributions are they making?
- What is the economic value to your business and the growth of your company, or are they just 'nice to have'?
- Are they increasing revenue and market share/mind share for your brand?
- Are they increasing overall profitability? That's where economic value comes into play.

When you dig a little deeper (should you have set up your marketing partnerships to be measurable activities for the business, as will be discussed in depth in chapter 7 on smart collaboration), you will find that your marketing partnerships will be contributing to the success of your business, not contributing at all or detracting from your business because so many crucial resources are being drained by them with very little return. You will find that some are performing better than others and would make for wonderful business case studies, while others waste valuable company time and are not worth the paper that was used to print up their respective partnership marketing agreements.

CONNECTION

Can we work together? Do we have similar cultures, values and practices? Do all participating brands consider this marketing partnership to be of equal importance to one another?

The second part of ECP is the 'C,' which stands for 'connection' and is the bridge that links the partner brands together, as it does individuals in a personal relationship. The connection therefore serves a crucial function as it's the part of ECP that ensures that all partner brands within the marketing partnership are integrated and truly sharing a common goal: to make the partnership work and to be as rewarding as possible. Without the connection, how can the marketing partnership realize the economic value that is sought by all parties? Without such a connection, what are the chances that the partner brands work to optimize the marketing partnership and work efficiently to realize the potential opportunities available? Without the connection you are more like a couple of brands that are aware of each other, but in reality, you don't know much about each other at all.

The connection is very important in determining whether or not you have a high level of ECP with your marketing partner(s). Partner brands that are well connected truly practice smart collaboration and maximize their efforts to work together, sharing their brands, budgets, staff, resources, systems, processes, sales channels, communications vehicles and customer-related activities. They develop a calendar of activities together, benefit from cost savings together and understand each other's business just as well as they do their own. They shouldn't drive their marketing activities independently and work internally from planning stages all the way to execution of the campaign as they might do when they are marketing directly.

As in a personal relationship, you cannot be connected or aligned in a marketing partnership if you do not know the other. It's important that partners know about each other's respective marketing practices, including how they generate revenue, the types of marketing vehicles used, the makeup of their customers and what markets their partner brands operate in. It is fundamental that you gain this understanding in order to maximize the partner program. It's virtually impossible to be connected as partner brands if you don't know all that much about each other's business. Only when you know a lot about each other do you have that all-important connection for a strong ECP.

To determine if you have a connection with a partner brand, you can ask the partner brand the following questions, and have them ask you the same questions:

1. Do you know how we generate revenue for our business?
2. Do you know which marketing communications vehicles and sales channels we use to acquire new customers?
3. Do you know how we retain our customers and facilitate repeat transactions?
4. Do you know about our products or services and any new ones that we are offering?
5. Do you know what markets we operate in and what regions we sell to?
6. Do you know what types of product enhancements we are developing for next year?
7. Do you know what our end customer profiles look like?

I appreciate that some of this information is confidential and that the partner brand may not be willing to just open up their marketing plan for you to read. This might be resolved easily by both parties signing a Non-Disclosure Agreement. However, if neither of you can effectively answer at least five out of the seven questions about each other's brand, then you are not connected. There is always an opportunity to address this. Get connected and build that bridge to work more effectively together.

PARTNERS

Is your company partner-friendly? Do you welcome partners into your business and are you ready to partner?

The third part of ECP is the 'P,' for partners. Partners are like people. If you're looking to have a positive, value-added and enriching relationship with them, you need to prove your worth. In addition, they need to do the same for you. They need to have the characteristics, personality and makeup of what you are looking for in a relationship. They need to excite you, or even 'wow' you, with their offering. You should miss them when they are not around, and vice versa.

Below, I describe the three types of partner (people) and their style of relationship.

Not Partner Friendly (Loner)

Some people are not ready to take on new friends and prefer to go it alone. They like being in control and they like marching to their own beat. They are not overly friendly and don't like the idea of having others in their lives infiltrating their inner circle. They don't need others, can get by on their own and don't see much value in changing their relationship style. They are happy with where they are and they can achieve their dreams without the involvement of friends. They don't require anyone to support their cause, get them to where they need to go, introduce them to something new or help them get to their appointments on time. They don't need a coach or instructor and can build out their own personal brand and broaden their horizons without the help of anyone. When it comes to choosing a partner, loners should be avoided. You will not get very far with them as your proposition will not mean much to them.

Somewhat Partner Friendly (What's In It for Me?)

These are people who like having others around them. They want to be part of an active social network and like having a large database of friends at their fingertips. They like knowing there is always someone they can have lunch with, see a basketball game with or attend a theatre event with. They like having a personal network to socialize with and have drinks with after work or for the occasional weekend coffee. They like knowing they have a lot of people around them who they can count on and fit into the different facets of their life. They are not so concerned with what their friends or the people in their personal network think of them, but more with what they are getting out of such relationships for themselves. They like having friends and people to count on and help them achieve their personal goals—and are usually less concerned with adding value to their friends' lives than having friends add value to theirs. They make for good partners but not great ones.

Partner Friendly (What's In It for Us?)

These are the people who want to help others with their goals while using their personal network to help get them to where they want to be. They are looking for people to add value to their life, but in turn want to add value to the lives of others. They get a particular joy out of helping someone succeed and seeing them do more with their life. These people truly benefit the most from their relationships. They understand the concept of giving: by helping others achieve their goals, they in turn will benefit. They have knowledge, skills and competencies they are willing to share to help others achieve on their own objectives—and they look for others who are also willing to share their knowledge, skills and competencies. They rely on their personal network to help them with their goals, and they want to add value to friends lives as well. They are more than willing to contribute to benefit others within their network. They typically make for great partners.

. . .

Like people, your partner brands have a business culture or personality of their own. Some will be very partner-friendly and integrate the partnership into many aspects of their company and practice partnership marketing throughout their business, while others may do this to a lesser extent. They may see the partnership as a 'nice to have,' but in no way a necessity or driver for them as they look to achieve their objectives.

When looking at prospective partner brands, you need to determine if they match your target profile (i.e., partner friendly). Your partners need to strategically fit with your objectives. You need to have common goals for the partnership and opportunities to leverage what each brings to the table. Ideally, you should provide each other with an opportunity to create long-lasting synergies and enhancements to each other's businesses. Not every relationship is equal, yet to increase your chances for success, it's crucial that you are willing to help each other's businesses and that you have the goods to deliver on that promise.

WHAT DOES IT TAKE TO ACHIEVE A SUCCESSFUL ECONOMIC CONNECTION AS PARTNERS?

Throughout the rest of this chapter, I will discuss the key factors for achieving a successful connection:

- Joint goal planning
- Skills and competencies
- Processes and technology
- Potential to generate incremental revenue

Joint Goal Planning

I often find that joint goal planning is the first place to start when exploring the opportunities to engage with a new marketing partner.

It's crucial to define the goals for any program, but its best in a marketing partnership to define and set those goals together, in advance of finalizing any agreement, in order to ensure that the partnership will meet both parties' objectives. There is very little or no sense at all in one partner brand doing all of the planning while the other brand sits back and has their own ideas about what they want to get out of the partnership.

Goal-Related Questions that You and a Partner Brand Should Ask

- What are your joint goals for the program?
- What does each party want to achieve from the partnership and what economic value are the organizations driving for each other?

- Do you have short-, mid- or long-term goals?
- Do you have a revenue target that you are trying to meet; and what is your partner's revenue target?
- If you are looking to acquire new customers, then outline how many you are looking to acquire and demonstrate the revenue that your partner brand could generate should they help you achieve that target.

Consider a marketing partnership that drives new customer acquisition for your business. You may decide that you want your partner brand to generate ten thousand new customers in a year and that you will accept nothing less. That's great, but what does your partner think? Are they aware of your goal? Do they understand what your expectations are and have they put forth plans to achieve them? Were they consulted, as part of the process of coming up with the target number? Based on their plans, do they believe they can deliver that for you? Perhaps they were using a benchmark of five thousand new customers or even fifteen thousand new customers.

The partnership relationship will get off on the wrong foot if goals are not defined and agreed upon. These are what set the stage for the partnership model of negotiation. This discussion is a very important part of whether or not a partnership will come together, and it plays a significant role in the negotiation strategy for how the partnership will be formed. Therefore, it is best to ensure you are up front with your goals and objectives from the beginning.

Some Joint Goal-Planning Points that You and Your Partner Brand Should Consider

- Take the time to make a list of the short-term and long-term goals for the partnership and be sure to align them to the needs of both you and your partner. Also list what you need to do to get there. If you want to acquire six hundred new customers from the marketing partnership and have signed a twelve-month partnership marketing agreement, that means

(continued)

that your plans have to get you approximately fifty new customers a month.

- Develop a partnership marketing activity plan together with your partner brand that includes all the necessary obligations, commitments and costs that each of the parties are going to take responsibility for in order to achieve the goals.
- Once you have set your goals and have an agreed plan in place, it is important to revisit them with your partner on a regular basis, at least once a quarter, to ensure they are still relevant. Add new goals as you need to and modify existing goals accordingly as market demand for your products and economies change.

Skills and Competencies

Before engaging in a marketing partnership with a partner brand, it is important to think about how you will manage the marketing partnership and what it's going to take to turn potential into reality. You will need employees with the right skills, competencies and capacity to make it happen, unless you plan on managing and developing the partnership on your own, although the same criteria apply.

You need to make a commitment that both your company's employees and your partner brand's employees will work on the marketing partnership and meet the goals that have been established for the partnership. Therefore, you need employees with good relationship management skills. They must be able to work effectively with their counterparts, who are employed by your partner brand, to ensure that obligations and business requirements are satisfied. For that they need to have the right balance between formal and informal communication skills and have the common sense to use the former or latter when appropriate.

Competencies also are required and range from the ability to use resources appropriately (time, budgets, people) to being able to interpret, evaluate and properly apply information. The employees must have strong interpersonal capabilities, work well with others, understand technology and use the systems required to manage the relationship.

Do you have the resources and the capacity to add a new partnership to you or your team's schedule? Factors that can have an impact on the partnership's success are the failure to assign key personnel or to provide adequate training that explains the nature and details of the partnership to your team. Do you have a process in place to manage the information flow when dealing with turnover of partner managers, in order to ensure that you provide a smooth transition of partner managers for your partner brand?

Can you assign a dedicated person to manage the program? In cases where a company has little or no experience with partnership marketing programs, it is quite often the case that a new program is assigned to someone who is told to 'keep an eye' on the program from afar. It is simply an add-on responsibility to their primary job responsibilities. This could end up leaving the program in disarray and sending a message to the partner brand that the program is not all that important. To avoid this, both companies involved in the partnership should assign key managers from the onset and give them ownership and accountability for the relationship.

As discussed above in the section on connection, you will need to learn about your partner brand's business, as they must do with yours. Gaining knowledge about their products and market, and sharing knowledge about what it is that you do, is crucial to achieving high levels of partner engagement and, ultimately, a strong ECP. Therefore, it is just as important to understand the skills and competencies that their resources bring to the partnership.

Key Points to Consider when Putting Together a Team with Your Partner Brand

- Ensure that the people to whom you assign responsibility for your partnership marketing program can work with others, influence decisions and work to mutually beneficial outcomes that meet company objectives.
- Ensure that the team resources identified understand that they are accountable for deliverables, see the 'bigger picture' of the partnership and understand how the performance of the marketing partnership

(continued)

affects the overall business or business unit so they get a feel for the importance and relevance of their role. Depending on the size of the partnership, consider incorporating the objectives of the partnership into the employee's performance goals.

- Be sure your resources are provided with the training that they need to improve their understanding of technology, systems and financial management, for example, so that they have the competencies to effectively manage the partnership marketing program.

Processes and Technology

In order to run your partnership marketing programs, you need processes and systems. Consider how the new partnership will affect the different areas of your business and how this new agreement will be communicated to the relevant business owners. If applicable, you will need to ensure that your customer service department and/or call center is aware of your offering. You will need to track progress and have a snapshot of how many conversions to your special offer were generated and be able to show your partner brand how much revenue they generated during the co-marketing campaign that they ran and for what period of time. You will need to be able to track that revenue in the first place and isolate it as a single line item so that you can analyze it independently. Forecasting capabilities are needed as well. Think about partner capabilities. Will your partner brand have all the systems and processes needed to run the partner program that you are going to pitch for them? Do you have a turnkey solution that you can deliver to them that is easy to implement or will you be setting up something from scratch?

Processes

In partnership marketing, processes are the routine sets of procedures that communicate, transact, fulfill and deliver a product from being made available via a special offer all the way to the end customer receiving the benefit from it.

Processes are necessary to achieve a strong ECP with your partner brand. Without them, your special offer will not be properly communicated to the partner brand's customers, your company will not be in a position to transact on the offer, you will not be able to fulfill offers correctly and you will not have smooth procedures for paying your partners for referring business your way. Further, you could be at risk of your customer never receiving the benefit promised to them in your offer. Whether you are a B2C or a B2B brand, processes are necessary.

The following example demonstrates the importance of ensuring that processes are established before the marketing partnership goes live. A company selling an in-home service partnered with a retailer who targeted homeowners with a distribution program that had an added-value component attached to it. The in-home service company leveraged the retailer's store locations to distribute flyers promoting their service, yet with a special value-add that tied into the retailer's brand. They offered the retailer's customers a $20 gift card, which could be used for purchases at the retailer's stores when the customer purchased the in-home service. The end customer picked up a flyer in-store, took it home and called the phone number on the flyer to book a service. They gave the call center agent the offer code from the flyer and, after the job was done by the in-home service company, the end customer received the $20 gift card by mail within two to four weeks.

The partner brands set the process as follows. Every two weeks, the in-home service company sent the retailer a list of all the customers who called in to book jobs with that offer code. The retailer then used the customer data to send out the $20 gift cards to the customers. The gift cards were paid for by the in-home service company, in exchange for receiving the distribution and promotion of their brand in the retail partner brand's stores.

A couple of months after the launch of the program, the in-home service company started to get a high level of calls to their call center from numerous end customers asking why they hadn't received their $20 gift cards yet. The call center was clearly in no position to address these customer complaints, so the issue was communicated to the partner manager of the program. How could this have happened, when the process had been clearly established?

Upon further investigation, it was confirmed that the retailer was receiving the end customer data and processing it, but the finance department at the retailer's head office had put a hold on the gift cards being issued to the customers because the company had not received payment from their partner brand (in-home service) that was funding the gift cards. The result was that the end customer was being penalized and suffered a sub-par customer experience because of the lack of process put into play to ensure that payments for those gift cards were moving from one brand to the other brand.

When drawing up your processes and how you want things to flow, it's crucial that you think of everything that needs to be done, because any glitch or breakdown in the process can bend your marketing partnership out of shape.

Technology

We need technology to power our marketing partnerships so that we can control and adapt our programs as needed. The complexity of your needs will vary, depending on the nature of the partnership entered into.

One of my clients recently asked me to investigate an opportunity for them to develop marketing partnerships with 'expert bloggers' in the small and medium-sized business space (SMB).

They believed that since their product was heavily targeted to the SMB owners, working with such bloggers could very well make for a positive endorsement of my clients' products and services to these bloggers' readers (being SMB owners). The rationale was that my client could leverage the influence and reach of these well-established experts. Interesting strategy, but just how feasible was it?

I started to break it down and quickly discovered that most of the bloggers that we would be partnering with did not have very sophisticated websites. Most of them were pretty basic and used a third-party blogging software provider like Wordpress or Blogger. They likely wouldn't be interested in adding an online store to their blogging site to resell my client's products and services. I shared this with my client and advised that, based on the current infrastructure, his idea did not appear feasible. In order to make it work, we would need to make it easy for the bloggers to implement.

We thought it over for a bit and then came up with a new angle. If we could provide them with a co-branded landing page that would sit on my client's website and would feature the offer, products for sale and both my client's brand and the partner brand, then all the expert blogger would have to do is link their website to that page and drive the traffic over. They wouldn't need to set up an e-commerce store on their site. My client could easily handle the transaction, track revenue generated from transactions that occurred from that page link and then give the blogger a percentage of the revenue generated from sales transactions from the traffic the blogger sent over (Distribution Marketing Partnership).

If you get creative and think about what you have to offer, sometimes you can overcome a lack of processes, technology and basic know-how to facilitate a successful marketing partnership for your brand. You may find that you can bring a solution to the table that will save your partner incurring additional costs to acquire a functionality or capability that you already have or can easily make available. As long as it's seamless and provides a great partner brand and end customer experience, then you can effectively leverage processes and technology already in place on one side of the marketing partnership and bring them over to the other side, thereby avoiding additional costs and additional development and learning time.

Key Points to Consider Regarding Processes and Technology to Strengthen Your Marketing Partnership

- Identify the key players and departments that are affected by your marketing partnership and develop a program flowchart so that you can assign responsibilities and create processes where needed.
- Ensure that all of the key players are clear on what their roles are and that you have the necessary checks and balances in place to stop aspects of the marketing partnership from slipping through the cracks.
- If you are not willing to incur costs to obtain the necessary technology to run your partner program, think about how you can leverage what your partner brand may already have available or about how you can split any costs that do need to be incurred.

Potential to Generate Incremental Revenue

You must enter into a marketing partnership negotiation having done some revenue projections based on what you already know about your prospective partner and their capabilities and assets. How many customers do they have? Once you have an idea of how many customers they have, you need to understand how they are going to represent or communicate your offering to those customers.

A company hired me to analyze an existing marketing partnership that they felt was not working for them. They were disappointed because, according to them, the partner brand was not doing their job and not generating any revenue for their business. When I looked into it a little closer, it appeared that the partner brand was a good fit strategically and had the right audience and customers to make the partnership work, with great potential for the partner brands to have a strong ECP. No wonder my client was shocked that the marketing partnership was not yielding any results. On a call set up with my client and the partner brand, I learned two very important factors that were limiting this marketing partnership from generating revenue:

1. The partner brand had two thousand customers.
2. The partner brand was not committed to marketing my clients' proposition and in the six months since forming the partnership had performed no marketing activity.

This isn't exactly the type of information that you want to learn about your partner brand *after* getting into a marketing partnership. With so few customers, how far could this partnership go? A response rate of two percent on a special offer (two percent being well above average response rates) would only result in forty customers taking advantage of the offer. Then, when you factor in that half of them will drop off after the free offer is over, you only have twenty new revenue-generating customers. My client, with almost two thousand clients of their own, had little to get excited about.

The second factor was even more challenging to address, because the partnership agreement did not address timing and frequency of the partner brand's marketing of my clients' proposition. My client had simply left it up to the partner to decide when and how to market the offer to their customers. As a result, aside from an initial email push to a segment of their customer base a week after they signed the deal, nothing had been done to revisit the marketing communications plan or strategy. With no marketing commitments and poor joint goal planning, this partnership was not displaying a high potential to generate revenue for my client and referral revenue for their partner.

It's important that you assess the opportunity, collect all the necessary information and check off all of the following boxes as you evaluate the potential for you and your partner brand to generate significant revenue for each other. Think of the following key factors, which will be discussed in more detail:

What to Evaluate When Considering a Partner Brand's Potential to Generate Incremental Revenue

❑ Products
❑ Offers and messaging
❑ Pricing
❑ Marketing vehicle, frequency and reach
❑ Recognizability

Products

Which of your products do you want to promote to your partner brand's customers, and which products of your partner brand do you want to promote to your customers? Do you understand your partner brand's mandate and strategy with their customers? Does your product support and supplement their existing proposition? Does your product enhance the value of their offering and is it relevant? If the answer to any of these questions is no, then you are not offering the right product to your partner. You may need to customize a product for their needs or even look at a new product category within your catalog. Or, it might not be the right partner brand for you.

Think about your customers and the products that you want to supplement your core offering. Think about what you want to make available to them that you currently don't own. Even if you're 'best of breed' for a given category or have a highly valuable proposition for your customers, partnering with a partner brand that is superior in their offering and great at what they do will only make your product stronger. Apple has a killer product in the iPad, but as great as they are at developing products and services for their customers, they still feature Google Maps and bundle it as the default map service on their tablet computer. While the Apple iPad is a highly compelling product in itself, Apple does not own a leading content program for every category they want to offer their iPad users. As a result, where they can partner, they will.

Offers and Messaging

Your offer to the customer ultimately buying the product should be highly compelling and interesting. Don't give a partner brand an offer that is not all that unique or different from what you typically offer to the market. You can't incentivize the partner brand to get behind an offer with primary placement and promotion in key marketing vehicles if there isn't something special in it for their customers. If your standard offer is ten percent off the first month, then making that very same offer in your partner marketing vehicles won't generate much sales traction for you. Furthermore, it will not encourage prospective partner brands to partner with you.

Think about it from the customers' perspective. Why would they purchase something from your partner by redeeming an offer that they can get somewhere else? Why would your partner brand want to be associated with an offer that isn't highly compelling or unique for their customers? We will discuss partner value propositions and creative propositions for the end customer later on in the book.

Your potential to generate significant revenue is highly dependent on the offer and the quality of that offer. On the flipside, if your partner brand is promoting an offer that doesn't have any perceived value attached to it, your program will likely underperform, even if it's well marketed. When I was at AOL, we gave Dell a special 'three months free' offer on hi-speed Internet to those who purchased a Dell computer. Dell really got behind the highly compelling offer. They marketed it extensively in their flyers, online advertising and the box that the computer came in. It was more compelling than our standard 'one month free' offer to the market. As a result, AOL generated significant customer registrations through this partnership.

When engaging in a co-marketing campaign, partner brands in a partnership marketing program need to decide, among other key things, who is in charge of messaging. Who is in charge of communicating with the customer and marketing the offer and program to them? What I typically advise on this front is that it's best for the brand that already has a relationship with their customers to lead the messaging efforts. Otherwise, it may come across as unwanted spam—and nobody wants to be perceived as a spammer. If you do communicate directly with your partner brand's customers, ensure that you have been given permission to do so and are presenting the offer as co-branded and that the partner brand has high levels of placement and promotion in your marketing communications. Again, it's best to position things this way to ensure that you will not be ignored but instead welcomed because you are a partner of someone that the end customer already interacts with regularly.

Pricing

How much does pricing matter in a marketing partnership? It matters a lot! In cases where you are not making an introductory offer (i.e., 1 month free!) available to the partner brand to promote to their customers, you need to ensure that the pricing you are making available is attractive. Without attractive pricing and price points that are highly competitive and reflect customer value, your marketing partnership will not go very far. You can sell products on your own for a given price, but if you make the exact same products available to partner brands at higher price points you are essentially knocking down the offer before it's even gotten started.

Try to avoid conflicting offers and find ways to give your partner brand a unique pricing proposition. For example, if your product is a subscription product and a prospective partner brand wants to promote it, but you don't want to cannibalize your existing business, maybe there is an opportunity to offer them a product that is sold with a one-time price. Perhaps you can create an alternative to the subscription payment model that you are offering to your customers, instead offering your partner the opportunity to sell a version of the product at a one-time price for lifetime use of the product. When you are marketing directly, you have much more control and can alter pricing as you see fit. That's not the case when you have a marketing partnership. You must give your partner everything they need to succeed, including special pricing or different pricing models to suit their needs and the needs of their customers—all while trying not to conflict with or compromise your other marketing programs.

Marketing Vehicle, Frequency and Reach

Marketing vehicles are used to communicate the offers and marketing messages to the customers of the partner brand. Without the right vehicles, it's likely that your partnership marketing program will fail to produce the desired results. Vehicle selection, therefore, is important. If you are relying on your partner brand to communicate a message on your behalf to their customers, then don't take for granted that they will use the most effective vehicles to do so. Ask questions about their website placements, email campaigns, in-store advertising, promotional direct mail and other vehicles that they may use as part of their customer communications strategy. Take it upon yourself to understand the successes and failures that each vehicle has achieved. If they are doing email marketing, understand their open rates (the percentage of those who receive an email and open it) and conversion rates (the percentage of those who open the email and subsequently convert to a paying customer by taking advantage of the offer being made). Compare these rates to other offers similar to the one you are making and get a handle on the metrics and what they determine to be a success.

The reality is that your partner brands know their customers, how they behave and the best way to target them. Your partner also knows the right frequency for communicating with their customers. Ask your partner to help position the free trial offer so that you generate effective sales traction, brand awareness or significant registrations.

You can have a great offer, but if it's communicated via the wrong vehicles and with limited frequency and reach, you may as well not run that partnership marketing program at all. Don't waste your time; you're not likely to achieve your desired results.

Steve Wallace, VP sales at CoastalContacts.com, says that "online marketing partnerships work best for our type of business as we are purely an online play." By selling product online via e-commerce only and not having a storefront, "we have generated much more success from our business by targeting customers online who are already comfortable with online environments and shopping online, and as a result, we have partnered with companies like Visa and their online 'Visa Perks' program as it's a great brand to affiliate to and Visa cardholders understand that Visa only partners with reputable brands . . . they can feel comfortable with their online purchase as one that is highly endorsed, making the end customer feel secure about their recent purchase (because the "Visa Perks" program is primarily marketed online to customers who want to shop online.)."

Recognizability

You need to determine if your partner brand elevates your brand because they are widely recognized and well branded, and if that is important to you. Widely recognized brands with good reputations can, among other things, enhance your brand and proposition and create credibility for your offering.

There is value in associating with certain brands, no matter what the relationship. Becoming an approved vendor, licensed partner or sponsor, or content provider for brands that have more customers, awareness and reach than you do can make a difference for your company, and help you grow awareness for your smaller, lesser-known brand. When thinking about affiliating with a given brand, you will want to understand their reach. Are they national or regional, for example? Perhaps you are well known in certain parts of the country, but lesser known in others. Partnering with a brand that has a strong presence in a geographic region can help you to become more well known in another part of the country more quickly and cost effectively.

• • •

We never know for sure whether or not a partnership marketing program is going to work over the long haul and provide incremental value to all partner brands. You can be certain, though, that if the partnership is not structured with an intention for both parties to succeed economically you likely have popped the air out of the balloons before they made it to the surprise party.

In order to achieve a strong ECP, you need to be realistic about your marketing partnership and its potential. The worst thing you can do is think that your marketing partnership has the ability to drive more business than it can generate. Forecast according to what makes sense and remove all of the emotion when creating such projections. If you are realistic and set expectations and goals with your partner brand around some achievable marketing objectives for the partnership, you will benefit from a strong ECP and dramatically reduce the chances of ruining the relationship. ECP is generated when all partner brands benefit, and expectations for the partnership have been met or exceeded because of the high level of economic results both parties have enjoyed.

I cannot understate the importance of ECP. You need to be economically connected to have a relevant, high-performing partnership that both you and your partner brand will care about. Our next chapter discusses what to look for in partner brands and why it's important to make sure that you qualify them before associating your brand with them.

5

Associating Your Brand

IN THE PREVIOUS CHAPTER, we discussed the importance of being economically connected as partners. In this chapter, we will highlight the components and characteristics you should look for when choosing a partner brand to be economically connected to. Think of it like composing a list of qualities that you would be looking for in a person that you would want to have a relationship with.

In an ideal world, what does your partner brand 'wish list' look like? What characteristics will their business need to have to support the goals for your marketing partnership, and how will you be able to support them in turn? There are a number of factors to evaluate at this stage of the partnership marketing process. The main criteria to explore are listed in the box starting below and are discussed in detail throughout this chapter.

What to Look for When Choosing a Partner Brand

- Customers—strong reach to the primary target market
- Relevance to your business—enhances offering to the primary target market

(continued)

- Size of opportunity
- Widely recognized brands
- Geography
- Mutuality and cooperation
- Credentials and trust
- Growth potential
- Legalities and channel conflict
- To White Label or Not to White Label
- Partner with winners
- Partner with an emerging channel
- Partner to establish credibility and confidence
- Partner with brands that offer products your customers want

CUSTOMERS—STRONG REACH TO THE PRIMARY TARGET MARKET

In marketing terms, your greatest strength is your mindshare, and if yours is strong, it's likely because your company has a unique ability to meet the needs and wants of customers by supplying them with the goods and services they are looking for at the right price point. That leads to greater opportunities to sell more products, leverage distribution channel networks and keep your customers loyal for longer. Customers are what every business is after. Without them, business doesn't exist. You can create products, package them, even put them up for sale on your website, but if nobody is buying from you, then your business isn't going to be worth very much and is much less attractive to a prospective partner brand. Ask yourself the following:

- What do your customers look like?
- Are the majority male or female?
- Aside from yours, what other products do they like to buy?
- Where do they live?
- What is their average income?
- Who are your best customers?

- Do they need to exhibit a certain type of behavior or skill set to want to buy your product or service? For example, do they need to be musicians or artists?
- Do they need to be at a certain life stage to have a need for your service? For example, do they need to be empty nesters?
- Do they need to be of a certain income level? For example, is their household income $100,000 or more for them to consider your service?
- Do they need to live in a certain city or country?

If you don't have a handle on who your best customers are, it's going to be difficult to engage in partnership marketing. It's not necessary to have a full-blown customer segmentation analysis done for your business, although it's recommended, but it is important that you have a general profile for your customers and their characteristics. You are going to want to partner with brands that have strong reach to the primary target market that you are after, but you can't determine those prospective brands if you don't know who your best customers are and understand why they are already buying from you. Establish who your primary target market is before you decide which partner brands to affiliate with. Your primary target market could be as general as 'small and mid-sized businesses' or as specific as 'first-time homeowners in major cities who have purchased homes valued at $500,000 or more and are moving in within the next thirty to sixty days.' Either way, you need to know this before you start thinking about which brands to associate with.

RELEVANCE TO YOUR BUSINESS—ENHANCES OFFERING TO THE PRIMARY TARGET MARKET

You can target your market either vertically or horizontally. Targeting a vertical market means that you are targeting potential businesses or consumers who have needs related to a specific industry or category like financial services, music, travel, medical or professional sports. If you are targeting horizontally, then your solution meets the needs of businesses or consumers within a wide variety of industries, not just one specific industry. When you start to develop your strategy for partnership marketing, you need to determine if your products are for a specific vertical market or if they meet the needs of a wider horizontal audience comprised of customers that can be targeted through strategic affiliations with brands in multiple industries. If your brand is 'horizontal,' you will need to determine which vertical industries are the best strategic fit for your products, so that you can prioritize accordingly. For example, are your products a best fit with the accounting or finance industries? Once you have figured that out, you can identify the brands within certain industries to target. We will discuss this more in chapter 6, Putting Partnership Marketing into Play. This is an important step because you will want to prioritize even further and select those brands that will trigger a more immediate response from your primary target market.

During a visit to my local grocery store, I noticed a brand of laundry detergent bundling an offer 'on pack' for a free carton of a new brand of orange juice when you purchased the laundry detergent. It appeared that you could take advantage of the offer on the spot. I tried to follow the logic and perhaps you can as well. Most consumers purchase their laundry detergent as well as their preferred brand of juice at the same grocery store, so hitting them up with a partner offer 'on pack' is pretty clever as they are already in the shopping environment that they need to be in to notice the offer and take advantage of it. Still, I was trying to get my head around how orange juice and laundry detergent were relevant to each other aside from accidentally spilling the juice on my shirt and then having to wash it. The link between orange juice and laundry detergent didn't seem to be a good strategic fit, and I started to wonder why the laundry detergent wouldn't have chosen to partner with a brand of fabric softener. My only conclusion is that both brands identified that customers who buy laundry detergent also buy juice, and affiliating with the laundry detergent was a great way to get existing juice drinkers to try the new juice. The manufacturers of the orange juice might have tried to partner with a brand of breakfast cereal, as orange juice has always been symbiotic with breakfast as opposed to laundry, but maybe it was not possible to get a breakfast cereal partner brand onboard. Maybe the partnership with the brand of laundry detergent would still create excitement around the laundry detergent brand and get the orange juice into the hands of the target audience.

A brand can target a vertical market as well as a horizontal market if their product meets the needs of both. Take Universal Music, for example. They sell music and look to target music lovers wherever they can. With the largest catalog of musical artists on the planet, Universal Music on MySpaceMusic only enhances the MySpace proposition. Universal Music can leverage the relationship to drive MySpace users to VEVO, their music video website, where users can check out new videos from new and existing artists and are then prompted to buy the songs on iTunes. That's an example of a music publishing company leveraging a distribution partnership to target music fans.

Universal Music also works with brands like Starbucks, which is not in the music business but is primarily in the coffee business. Starbucks customers can hear music from their favorite artists in-store and then purchase the music at the Starbucks counters in CD format. Universal realized that music fans are coffee drinkers as well, and that they could market their music to a wider horizontal audience by having their artists be heard at Starbucks locations.

It doesn't matter if your products meet the needs of a vertical market, horizontal market or both. What does matter is that the marketing partnership that you facilitate is relevant to the businesses that you are partnering with and enhances the core value proposition to the primary target market.

SIZE OF OPPORTUNITY

Partnership marketing programs take time to develop and launch. You need to prospect your partner brands, decide on the value proposition, sign the agreement, agree to launch plans, produce creative and collateral, and then manage the programs once they go live. Determining the size of the opportunity requires taking a detailed look at what your partnership can achieve.

If you are a brand that sells a product to a business, for example, and have a choice to partner with two associations that cater to small business owners, where Association A has a hundred thousand members and Association B has fifty thousand members, which one would you choose? Likely if you could partner with only one of them, you would choose Association A because they have twice as many members. Most people would make the same choice. However, with the limited information provided in this example, a more fitting response might be 'it depends.' After making your choice and finalizing your marketing partnership, your partner brand (Association A) advises that their plan is to email ten thousand of their members with your offer and that they are not committing to anything more than that. You are caught off guard, but as the agreement is finalized, you go ahead with the program. The result here is not a bad one, but is it the best opportunity available to you given that you had to choose to work with one association only? What if the smaller association (Association B), with half the number of members, had planned to email all of their members with your offer? That is what you potentially missed out on. When partnering, it's not just about the size of the organization or partner brand that you are going to work with, it's about the size of the opportunity available to you.

Calculating the size of the opportunity requires gathering the right information from the prospective partner brand. You need to find out how many customers they have, as well as how far their reach is as a brand and what frequency of interaction each of their marketing vehicles has. Which products and offers do your customers value the most, and therefore, which ones should you be pushing most as a partner brand? Zappos.com, a leading online seller of footwear, works with Overlay.TV to produce interactive videos for popular footwear products from partner brands that they sell on their websites. The videos allow viewers to shop directly from them, and they can be shared on blogs and social media profiles. Zappos plans on offering this for all partner brands, but they are starting it off with Nike as Nike presents a sizable opportunity to test the technology and launch it (Marketingvox.com, November 30, 2009).

WIDELY RECOGNIZED BRANDS

Everyone wants to work with widely recognized brands or, as they are often referred to, 'category leaders.' It poses a nice opportunity for partnership. If you can get a partnership marketing program going with one of them, you will certainly be able to benefit from their market position, brand awareness, large customer base and ability to create high levels of visibility and sales traction for your brand. However, my experience has been that large, well-established brands like to work with other large, well-established brands and typically partner only with other market leaders. As with anything else, there are exceptions, but size matters to market leaders. The ability to drive significant volume, value and profit from the marketing partnership will be seen as something they can do only with a partner brand that is also considered a market leader.

These widely recognized brands are prestigious and drive their industries forward. In many cases, they do use partnership marketing strategies and tactics within their business, but they also don't always need the help or want to give any help. If they have more customers than any of their competitors and are leading their market, then they may not feel that they need you or your company as a partner brand to help them with their marketing objectives. They may have the philosophy that they are sitting in the driver's seat and taking their industry forward and, as a result, they can handle it on their own. Therefore, it may be good to partner with the second or third or fourth brand for the given category. After all, their goal is to become number one, and if you have a strong value proposition to offer them, they could be more receptive to your offering and to seeing the benefit to their business.

Finally, you need to think about how meaningful your program will be to these widely recognized category leaders. Are they too big for you? Will your partnership marketing program not get the attention that it deserves and fall through the cracks? If the program is ignored and left to sit in limbo, you will have invested a considerable amount of time, money, resources and energy on it, and you will receive no return for that investment. You also will have a high opportunity cost of not partnering with another brand that could have had a much larger positive impact on your business.

Tips for Smaller Brands Wanting to Partner with Larger Brands

- Larger brands might be large, but that doesn't mean that they are great at what you do—present your proposition and the benefits of it.
- Demonstrate how your value proposition aligns to theirs. Show them why your product is complementary and will enhance theirs and support and supplement their offering.
- To engage the larger partner brand's customers, consider funding a contest or sweepstakes.

GEOGRAPHY

In this digital and wireless world we are living in today, where technology allows us to connect easily from one side of the planet to the other, the necessity for partner brands to be in the same geographic region is widely outdated. In fact, it has been for years, but with the increase in online usage and its penetration across the globe—together with what constant connectivity has brought with it—there is less and less need for partner brands to limit themselves to their own geographic market. They do not have to develop partnership marketing programs with companies that they can meet with face to face. Sure, the meeting in person component is a nice part of relationship building, and meeting in person (even if only a few times a year) can certainly increase opportunities to maximize the program and take the relationship to the next level, but it isn't necessary.

In today's world, you can be based in Paris and easily form a three-way partnership marketing program with a brand headquartered in Los Angeles and another brand headquartered in Shanghai, especially if much of the program will take place online. With more and more marketing campaigns and marketing budgets moving to online or digital channels, leveraging websites, email campaigns, social media pages, affiliate programs and e-commerce is more relevant than ever before. Furthermore, even if you are in a different geographic market than your partner brand, you will have more visibility and transparency to the program than in the pre-digital world. You can actually see your placements, be included on email communications with your partner offer and use online collaboration tools in real time to track progress and performance. It's all at your fingertips.

MUTUALITY AND COOPERATION

In a marketing partnership, the partner brands are typically bound by a series of obligations that they each must undertake to drive the partnership marketing program forward. The reality is that if your partner brand doesn't value what it is that you are bringing to the partnership, then they likely will fall short in adhering to their obligations, even if they agreed to become a partner in the first place. You will find yourself chasing them to get things done, question-ing the level of commitment and cooperation they have for the program, and starting to wonder whether it's all worth it. We discuss pitfalls and the concept of 'cutting the cord' or 'pulling the plug' on your marketing partnership in chapter 7, but you can do yourself a favor by scoping your prospective partner brand before such a decision becomes necessary.

Is your partner brand providing accessibility to their business in a conve-nient and open way? Is accessing their offer something that your customers would deem to be a good customer experience? Does your partner brand value your offer? Are they cooperating in marketing it effectively to their customers and leveraging whatever marketing vehicles they have with regular frequency? In a marketing partnership, both brands are mutually dependent on each other and, as a result, they are more than just bound by their obligations to each other. They need to effectively carry out their commitments to achieve success from the program. It's a joint effort, where the partner brands work together for a common purpose to receive the benefits that the marketing partnership has to offer. Those benefits are usually economic in form and are the reason that the businesses developed their association with each other in the first place. Get a sense for your prospective partner brand. Find out if they already have experience working with other partner brands and learn how their other programs are performing. Understand who is going to be in charge on their end of making sure that cooperation exists and that obligations are carried out in a timely and professional manner.

What to Ask Prospective Partner Brands About Their Existing Partner Programs

- Which programs are working best? Which are driving the most economic value?
- What makes the most successful programs work? Why have some pro-grams worked better than others, and how can we emulate that success?
- What were the objectives of your last few partner programs, and did you meet or exceed them?

CREDENTIALS AND TRUST

Exhibiting a basis of confidence and belief in your brand is going to be the trigger that determines if other brands will want to work with you. Just as you will want to know about your potential partner brand's reputation, your partner brand will want to know that if they partner with your company and brand, their brand's reputation will not be compromised by entrusting you with the responsibility of servicing their customers once they have referred them to you. You will need to provide them with that reassurance, and ensure that your brand's reputation is good, if not great. In our super-connected world, it's easy for anyone to research articles, feeds and news stories that relate to a prospective partner brand and check up on recent announcements that the business may have made or, potentially, announcements from existing partner brands of that company. It's possible that you have a contact that knows someone who knows you or someone else who works for the same organization and therefore can get the goods on how you operate with the click of a mouse or a simple text message.

Giving up control or responsibility, especially when it comes to your customers and marketing to them, falls out of the comfort zone for most businesses. You will need to trust in your partner brands' product or service, and their ability to deliver it and stand by it over time, just as your partner brand will need to trust you. Putting someone else in charge or assigning that responsibility can be done comfortably only with partner brands that demonstrate some terrific credentials and are highly trusted by their customers, partners, suppliers and the general public.

GROWTH POTENTIAL

Business growth in the context of partnership marketing is typically associated with the ability of your partner brand to drive volume, value, revenue, profit and opportunity for your business and vice versa. As discussed in chapter 3, there are several ways to increase revenues for your business and partnership marketing can play a significant role in all of them. Still, it's important to know that your partner brand does have the ability to get you there. It starts with understanding how stable their business is.

How to Assess Growth Potential in a Prospective Partner Brand

- Are they growing or contracting?
- Do they face a lot of competition or are they a market leader?
- What are their key growth metrics, such as revenues, profits, number of employees, office locations and product launches?
- What are the trends in their industry, and where does your potential partner brand fit in?

If your prospective partner brand is in 'cut back' mode, it's likely not good timing to get into a marketing partnership with them. They are likely so preoccupied with their current struggles to not 'go under' that the prospects of anything related to an extension or expansion of their marketing activities is not on the radar. Even if you are successful in negotiating a partnership marketing program for your brand, you will still find challenges in getting that incremental value that you are looking for, because the partner brand may only be able to put limited resources towards delivering on what's required to make your partnership a success. You will definitely want to be sure that their business is healthy and that the future of their business supports the growth potential you are looking for in a partner brand.

LEGALITIES AND CHANNEL CONFLICT

Some industries have pretty strict marketing laws, and adherence to and observance of those laws is absolutely necessary to avoid negative legal ramifications for a business. In some markets, you cannot legally force a consumer to purchase your product to gain the right to access a ticket for a contest promotion and, as a result, businesses must leave contests open with no purchase required. In other markets, you need to market goods and services in the country's official language(s), and you may need to take on the costs of preparing copy and translation for messaging, as the partner brand may not want to incur those costs. Some industries don't allow cross-marketing of other services to their customers and are restricted by what they can market and promote. In some cases, the word 'free' can be used only in offer messaging in certain contexts, with restrictions around how it's presented to the consumer. There's lots to think about, and this should come into play when selecting partner brands— you need to understand their business as well as you do your own to maximize the opportunity at hand and not be forced to abandon your marketing plans because of what you are technically 'not allowed' to do.

Distribution channel conflict can occur when a given brand already has a commitment to work with a set of partner brands and already has special offers in place with them. If they sell their products through existing partner programs, you will need to be sure that the offer they are making available to you and your brand is highly compelling. You will want your customers to view that offer as being unique and something that they can't get anywhere else, especially at one of the brand's other partner brands' websites. There are creative ways of not conflicting with other partners by making the offer just as valuable, but by changing the product or simply making certain offers through specific or discrete channels only or when another product is purchased.

Channel conflict is not good for your business or your partner's business, so you need to understand what they have in the market and what their future commitments look like before proceeding. For example, if you are a retailer, you may already have a special offer with a leading credit card or financial services company for their customers. Say you have been approached by one of their competitors (another leading credit card or financial services company) to make an even better offer available for their customers. Bringing on one of their competitors as a partner may upset the partner brand that you are already working with for the financial services category and would cause serious channel conflict. Therefore, before you engage partner brands that are directly or indirectly competitive with each other, you need to be sensitive to the fact that the partner brand you brought in first will likely not be happy that you are working with a competitor of theirs.

TO WHITE LABEL OR NOT TO WHITE LABEL

Partnership marketing, like any other type of marketing, involves an element of branding. If you are getting together with another brand, then you need to consider how you want to brand the new proposition that is resulting from your joint effort. Is your brand going to be front and center? Will it be co-branded? Will the partner's brand be the only brand advertised? What is the right way to brand this new offer, product or service that you are making available? Well, it depends on many factors, including circling back to what the objectives are for the marketing partnership.

The decision to white label (which means to offer a solution to a partner, but have them put only their brand on it) and make the product available under the partner's brand only, may be made simply because the partner brand wants it that way and you actually have no choice in the matter. Given that it may not meet your objectives for the program, you must decide how badly you want to partner with the other brand. Will white labeling bring about as much, if not more, success? If the partner brand has the stronger brand and their customers are quite brand loyal, and you have a relatively unknown brand, then it just might be the right thing to do. The last thing that you should be doing is slapping your brand all over the packaging (in this case) and hindering your chances for success.

As in every aspect that makes up your partnership marketing program, branding must be considered. The wrong branding decision can have a serious impact on your chances for success. Branding decisions should be based on achieving the key success metrics for the program and, ultimately, your business objectives. If you are looking to build your brand and 'brand equity' in an effort to one day sell your company based on being the well-known market leader in your category, then you may want to ensure that your brand is front and center. If your goals are more to drive immediate revenue and you can benefit by having other brands white label the solution, then that is OK as well. Just be sure that you get the right value in exchange for allowing them to go the white labeling route. Ensure that you receive an incremental fee or some other kind of benefit for allowing them to do so.

Sometimes white labeling can only take you so far. Say you have an electronics store and you sell white label flat screen TVs, DVD players and computer monitors with your brand or a new brand on them that you own the rights to, which you create for sale in your store only. This could very well be an integral part of your sales and marketing strategy to offer lower-end products to your customers as an alternative to traditional well-known branded products. Still, how far can you go with that? By making a certain amount of shelf space available and carrying less of Samsung, LG, Sony, Panasonic, Toshiba and Sharp products, to name a few, can you really grow your market share in the space? Will not carrying Apple or Dell computers and focusing on lesser-known brands really drive sales and increase opportunities for your business? How much in-store presence do you give to these brands now and is that really what your customers are looking for? Is it the only way you can compete?

White labeling products and services for partner brands can be an effective strategy to gain distribution with partner brands who may only want to offer their customers products and services under their own brands and not yours. If you are less concerned about being a destination brand, having your own relationship with end customers and increasing your brand awareness, then white labeling your products to another brand can be an effective way for you to associate and affiliate your offering with other brands that would otherwise not be a possibility if you want to brand it as your own. Let's look at some case studies that explore this issue.

Some Case Studies
Wal-Mart and Dell

Take Wal-Mart, for example. In recent years they have made an aggressive push to build out their electronics category within their stores. They wanted to offer everything under the sun, from MP3 players and digital cameras to personal computers, and to compete with the likes of Best Buy, Radio Shack and others. The reason Wal-Mart wanted to do this is simple—consumer electronics is one of the largest consumer categories on the planet and they wanted to be part of it. Given the socio-demographic of their customers and more and more people wanting cost-effective options for purchasing their favorite electronic toys, Wal-Mart figured that they could not only enter the category but be a leader within it. Given that they are one of the largest retailers of DVDs and music CDs in the world, it was a no-brainer.

Still, for Wal-Mart, they had to go about it in the right way. The reality is that some customers are going to walk into your store demanding certain product brands that they are familiar with and wanting to see those there. For example, the appetite for Dell computers (which once sold direct to the public only and not via retailers) is so strong and an association with their brand is so great that selling Dell computers can bring legitimacy to you and your business as a category leader overnight. So, Wal-Mart made a priority of bringing a low-end Dell model into their stores as part of their offering. Not only is this a way for Dell to increase their distribution, but it's a win for Wal-Mart as well. The downside in Wal-Mart not having the Dell brand (or any other major brand, for that matter) in-store and white labeling their own brands is that the product life cycle is very short in the computer space, spanning only thirteen to fifteen weeks. If Wal-Mart were to invest in their own brand and it did not result in sales traction and uptake with their customers, they would be stuck with a lot of product that they would ultimately take a big loss on. Wal-Mart is not only benefiting by partnering with another world-class brand like Dell but they are also minimizing their own business risk and ensuring that they do everything possible to maximize inventory turns.

For Dell, there are numerous advantages as well. The partnership with Wal-Mart is more than one that allows them to create greater brand awareness by affiliating with the world's largest retailer; it's about Dell reaching an end customer that they would not neccesarily be able to reach online or by phone. Ten years ago, Dell was predominantly selling computers to businesses. Now they want more and more of their customers to be consumers, so it's necessary to offer machines at better price points with more up-to-date technology and to target consumers who are looking to add that third, fourth or fifth computer or 'screen' to what they already have at home. There came a time when Dell needed to sell through Wal-Mart and be part of what they are doing. It's worth it to Dell as they can still create direct relationships with customers as they did when they strictly marketed and sold their products directly to the public. They can do that via their registration and warranty programs, for example.

By having customers register their products with Dell (even if bought from Wal-Mart, or another retailer), the company can collect valuable customer data and leverage it as an opportunity to cross-market and sell additional Dell products like printers and other peripherals to the customers who purchased their computers at Wal-Mart. The partnership acts as a lead generation vehicle for Dell and drives incremental revenue beyond the immediate transaction or sale they make to Wal-Mart customers.

Competitors like Hewlett-Packard, for example, leveraging a direct sales model of their own and competing with Dell, have practically forced Dell to consider other options like selling through retailers to maintain their market share and even continue to grow it. Sometimes, more than anything else, marketing partnerships happen out of necessity and as a result of the dynamics and changes in the competitive market.

Amazon

In Canada, Amazon (Amazon.ca) recently launched a 'Home & Garden' category for their online shoppers to take advantage of another huge industry that is primarily dominated by the Home Depots and Targets of the world. In a similar effort, Amazon is looking to offer name-brand products, much like they have done in other categories that they have been successful with, and establish themselves accordingly. Partnering with brands that already have customer appeal and are well known makes it easier for an online retailer to overcome the notion that most people would not purchase a patio chair or vacuum cleaner online. It's one thing to purchase a DVD or a book, but a vacuum cleaner? The reality is that the decision to sell highly regarded brands does more than establish Amazon within the category; it allows them to have success with it. If someone finds a brand of vacuum cleaner that they are looking to buy priced for less than in the store, then they just might buy it online and not have to deal with the time, travel and inconvenience of running out to a store to buy it.

PARTNER WITH WINNERS

Partner with winners, and avoid partnering with brands that have seen their better days or simply don't appear to have a strategy in place that will allow them to be around in the future and are ultimately on a path to nowhere.

Partnering with companies that sell cheap long distance plans that are being squeezed by major telecommunications companies who give unlimited free long distance as part of their product bundles and by newer applications like Skype are not good partners because their market shares and customer bases are shrinking, not growing. Video rental businesses are being replaced by video-on-demand and cell phones are being replaced by smartphones. Go to your local Blockbuster in the United States and ask them if their net number of new subscribers is increasing year on year. I would be pretty surprised to hear them say yes, and as for a younger demographic, they would have lost that market altogether if not for their entry into the gaming sector.

Want to be working with a manufacturer of flat screen TVs to target consumers in the North American market? Think Panasonic or Samsung. If it was twenty years ago, and you were looking at the TV category, you might be thinking Zenith or JVC. Who has the better future ahead of them in the apparel space? Lululemon or the Gap? It's not what you could have done for me fifteen years ago, but what you can do for me over the next fifteen years. That is what you need to consider when you are relying on a partner brand to increase your chances for success in your business.

Questions to Ask Yourself to Determine if a Partner Brand Is a Winner

- How are sales of your products? What is the trend—upward, flat or downward?
- Who are your competitors and what percentage market share do you have?
- What products or services are you developing for the market? What needs will they address? How are you positioned for the future of your product category?

You want to be working with brands that are on the move—not necessarily the largest player in the category or the most popular brand, but a company that is growing and moving upward and onward. Do the math. If they are shrinking, then so does your opportunity with them. If they are not 'on trend' or ahead of the trend, then where will that place you? If they don't demonstrate innovation, then where will they be two years from now? Again, you need to understand your prospective partner brand's business just as well as you do your own, if not even better. Why? Because your success is dependent on them! Ever hear the expression "it's all about me"? Well, when doing partnership marketing, "it's all about them." You need to understand their products, services, marketing and media assets, what they do well and what they don't do so well and what is posing a threat to their business. You need to understand their strategic priorities, if you will ultimately be a 'nice to have' partner or a strategic partner that is tied to the core of their business and that can help determine the outcome for success.

When looking at prospective partner brands that you would like to work with, don't stop at how big they are or the appearance of the overall size of the opportunity and form conclusions based on those two things alone. Some companies are so big that they may not put you at the top of their priority list, leaving you months and years away from launching your partner program with them and losing valuable time in the process.

Look at them in the context of what opportunities they can bring to your business and what you can do for them. What are the top three things that you can bring to the table for them in a marketing partnership, and what are the top three things that you would like to see them bring to you? What is it about their brand that can bring these things to you, and what is it about your business that adds value for them and helps them better sell or market their products? If you were looking for retailers to offer their customers one hundred free digital music downloads from your catalog of independent artists that you represent, would you partner with the likes of Circuit City, Kmart and HMV, or would you be better off working with Best Buy, Wal-Mart and iTunes? If you are looking to bundle a unique toolbar that sits in the Internet browser and make it available with new laptops, would you bundle it with Acer and Sony or would you offer it to Dell and Hewlett-Packard?

It's not that there are bad options in the aforementioned examples, but do your research on who is selling more products and leads in market share for their respective categories and you will quickly gain some perspective on who is doing what in their line of business. Again, big is great, because large brands with lots of customers, marketing presence and brand power are attractive when you think about what they can do for you and your products or services, but it's more important that you partner with winners that will do something for you. It's not about what they can do, but what they will do and what they will make available to you in terms of marketing vehicles and visibility for your products as a partner brand. More importantly, are they winners heading in the right direction? A large brand that doesn't prioritize the partnership and has seen better days will not be as effective a partner brand as a smaller brand that has a great future ahead of it, will make your product or service a core part of their offering and will provide high levels of exposure for you as they grow.

Choose a Partner Brand that Has a Market Share Within Your Target Market

Another thing to consider, besides the overall market share, is the market share within the target market that you are after. If you are looking to only target female tweens, then you need to partner with a brand that has those customers in place. If you are looking to target people that may be renovating their homes, then you need to ensure that the partner brand can effectively reach that audience. If you want to offer your proposition to adventure travelers, then maybe it's a good idea to stay away from a cruise line that only features 'party cruises' to the Caribbean. Wait a minute, did I not say partner with winners? Yes, I certainly did, but I want to add to that—it's not just about partnering with winners but partnering with winners that speak to the same audience that you want to be speaking to.

McDonald's wins during most economic cycles, and even thrives in periods of recession, but if you are a luxury brand, perhaps it's not the best fit. McDonald's is partnered with Monopoly. Why? McDonald's is the most successful quick-service, 'family-oriented' burger restaurant on the planet and Monopoly is one of the most popular selling, 'family-oriented' and highly recognized board games on the planet. How can that not work? They've got websites, in-store point of purchase displays, posters on the walls and on-pack promotion. They've got a strong consumer value proposition—play to win cash. Who doesn't want cash? And, they've tied your opportunities to win into having to buy more sodas, burgers and french fries in order to gain those much-needed monopoly pieces that are required in order to play. Not only is the game an opportunity for McDonald's to increase transactional value from each customer purchase, but it's a driver to increase frequency of interaction and the number of transactions that a customer may make, as discussed in chapter 3. The more transactions, the more customers get to play.

I think it's pretty brilliant and, if anything, the association with Monopoly provides McDonald's with an opportunity to block out their competitors and keep their customers loyal for longer. For Monopoly, why not? It's an opportunity to advertise, promote and engage the McDonald's customer with their brand and to have the customer experience the brand firsthand by playing to win cash. Furthermore, and more importantly, they are engaging a demographic and audience that would see value in spending the $15 or $20 on one of their board games in the future.

The only flaw I saw when I visited the website where you actually play the game was that there wasn't a strong call to action to purchase Monopoly board games. I am not sure if that was part of the deal, and given that Monopoly sells their games through many different types and sizes of retailers, it could very well be the result of wanting to avoid any channel conflict with retail partners like Toys"R"Us or Wal-Mart. Many reasons may explain the setup of the partnership, but it is important to consider each potential opportunity and to ask your partner brand to make it available. You never know what you can get if you do not ask!

Know the Viability of Your Partner Brand's Products

Also think about the products that the partner brand has made available to you to partner with. Do their products have a future? Are they going to be viable in a year from now? Rubbermaid manufactures storage and organization products for your kitchen, closet and garage. They have containers to store your leftovers in as well as shelving that can keep your storage room organized. They also have a line of outdoor products like garbage and recycling bins, and storage sheds to keep the bins in. They are great products and I actually own a few of them. Well made and built to last—they're certainly of the quality that you would expect from a brand like Rubbermaid.

Let's say you are running a junk-removal service and want to make a special offer to homeowners who during spring cleaning, moving or renovation may have a need for your service. Your strategy is to bundle the special offer as an on-pack coupon that will go on highly relevant products that target the audience that you are after: homeowners. Given their product offering, there's no better brand than Rubbermaid, right? Sure. They have all kinds of products that homeowners would buy every year if not more than once a year.

You take a look through their product catalog, and when you find their garbage and recycling bins you like the tie-in between junk removal and throwing out the trash and recycling. From a behavioral perspective, the actions of throwing out trash and having someone with a big truck show up at your home to remove some larger unwanted items is certainly relevant. So you go ahead with a pitch to Rubbermaid on a bundling program to drive traffic to your service with a special offer on-pack coupon to be bundled with every garbage and recycling bin.

Sounds great, right? Well, it depends on where in the world the program will be launched. In North America, that sort of partnership marketing program would die a quick death before ever getting off the ground. In the market that I live in, cities are now standardizing garbage and recycling removal. They actually insist that the homeowners who reside in their municipalities use the garbage and recycling bins that they are now providing 'free of charge,' with a minimal annual cost for a larger unit. These new bins have been custom built to fit the new technologies that the garbage and recycling trucks have where they pick up the bins and dump them via a mechanical arm as opposed to having an individual do it. Furthermore, the city can regulate just how much garbage and recycling people get rid of every week. As a result, this trend is likely to force companies like Rubbermaid to shift away from manufacturing such products as demand and necessity dwindles, and what you have essentially done is partnered with a product or designed your partnership marketing bundling strategy around a product line that is soon to be controlled by hundreds and thousands of municipalities across your territory and market. Partnering with products that have a short life cycle, or ones that are being phased out because of changes in regulations and legislation, is not worth it as the products will not provide you with an opportunity to succeed and meet your objectives.

Of course, if such an initiative has not yet hit your city, this could be a strong partnership opportunity. The point is to think about the product or technology that you are considering as a partner brand before investing the time in building a partnership that might be flawed from the outset because of changes in industry standards or other factors.

PARTNER WITH AN EMERGING CHANNEL

I think it's pretty clear that buying your milk at Wal-Mart, your pot holders at Amazon and your music at iTunes would have seemed pretty unrealistic ten years ago, but it's more than ever a reality today. If we think about this in the context of marketing channels and buying channels, more and more retailers or e-commerce sites are making more and more products available for purchase through the Web, mobile apps, catalogs and phone than ever before. Long gone are the days when you had to leave your house for a day of shopping and go to your local retail store to get your hands on a new book from your favorite author. Many retailers are 'multi-channel' marketing and offering customers the ability to purchase from them in many different ways.

In light of that, new businesses are emerging, such as the business of selling contact lenses online in the American and Canadian markets. Coastal Contacts has been doing this for years in other markets and has become the partner of choice for leading manufacturers and suppliers of contact lenses who want to get their products out to the public. According to Steve Wallace, vice president of sales at Coastal Contacts, as demonstrated in many markets around the globe, it's apparent that contact lens customers like the convenience of ordering online by filling out their prescriptions electronically and then getting their lenses delivered within forty-eight hours to their home, office or any delivery address provided. Wallace goes on to emphasize this point by highlighting the convenience for travelers who might have left home without their lenses and now find themselves on a beach in Florida needing a pair of lenses quickly and efficiently. Furthermore, the lenses are cheaper because of the massive inventories that the company carries, from a range of suppliers, in their Vancouver-based warehouse. Wallace confirms that there is a lot of work to be done to further establish the company in the contact lens market, but already they are the leading online seller in Canada and are seeing massive amounts of growth from month to month.

Let's put that into context from a partnership marketing point of view. What could the future look like? As online penetration increases and as buying habits change and comfort in buying contact lenses online continues to climb, making it more and more the norm, what does that mean for targeting consumers of eye care products? What it could very well mean is that as a shift in behavior occurs for a given category (like eye care), new opportunities for partnership develop. Given that it's already more cost-effective to acquire new customers online, and targeting specific audiences based on profiling is more effective online, could this not be a huge opportunity for companies who sell products within the eye care category, or related to the eye care or health care category, to target a very established base of the right consumers that is already more than comfortable buying online? Given that this is where it's all heading, should it not be the right thing to partner with emerging channels and businesses that are increasing their online share of the market as opposed to the more traditional channels?

A look into trends could show you that certain channels for selling and distribution that did not exist, and in some cases were even unheard of years ago might be emerging today—and, you might want to be aware of it. You might want to partner with those companies that are changing the industry, revolution-izing and innovating as opposed to sticking to their old ways. You might want to partner with the likes of a channel that is committed to evolving their business to meet the demands and needs of customers, as opposed to partnering with a brand that may not even be around five years from now because their channels and methods for selling and distributing products are no longer attractive.

PARTNER TO ESTABLISH CREDIBILITY AND CONFIDENCE

Another benefit of leveraging smart marketing partnerships and collaborat-ing with others is the credibility edge it can give. You may very well have a strong value proposition but need something to gain credibility with a group of customers that you might be targeting. Sometime the target feels something is missing in giving them the confidence that your business is credible and that you are not only great at what you do, but one of the best (if not the best) at doing it. You need to incorporate a partner brand into the mix in some way, shape or form that allows your potential customers to say, "we can trust in this—let's go with it."

Establishing credibility and confidence is not only for new start-up businesses. A brand like Tim Hortons has for a long time held their position at the top of the coffee market with well over seventy percent of the market share in Canada. In the United States, though, it's a much different story. Tim Hortons is pretty much a regional brand and much less of a national player. It's only available in certain states, predominantly in the northeast. Coffee is a competitive business with the likes of Starbucks, Dunkin' Donuts, Seattle's Best, McDonald's and a whole host of others on a regional and national level fighting for market share and promoting offers to encourage consumers to switch to their brand and try a new brew in an effort to hook them and keep them for life. The coffee market is a tough one to crack, and it's not just about appealing to consumer tastes and likes for a certain flavor of coffee. It's about distribution, pricing and becoming a product that customers want to affiliate and associate with. It's hard to come into a war with so many established players and have to build up your arsenal all on your own with limited resources.

So, having said that, what are the costs associated with marketing and selling your proposition if you don't absorb all of the costs on your own? Well, think of it this way. You share the staff, you might share the cost of distribution, you share a portion of the rent and you share the operational and utilities costs associated with running the store every day. Not only do you share all of those costs, but you are sharing them with a well-established brand that already has high levels of footfall traffic coming through their doors every day.

The result is that Cold Stone Creamery becomes a marketing partner of Tim Hortons in Canada and vice versa in the United States. The result is that you're increasing the number of transactions and overall transactional value per customer on every visit by increasing mind share and adding an offering in a new category. You can then bundle the products 'coffee and ice cream' for cheaper and capture a larger portion of the customer's wallet because they are no longer walking down the street for ice cream or coffee. The advantages are numerous, the benefits outweigh the costs and the opportunities are endless. That is what partnering with an established, strong brand in a given market that you want to play in can do.

PARTNER WITH BRANDS THAT OFFER PRODUCTS THAT YOUR CUSTOMERS WANT

Do you know what your customers want? Have you done a survey on what they are looking for? Don't be afraid to ask them. It's easy to come up with partner brands on your own and assume what your customers may want, but without asking them, how will you know for sure?

Determining what your customers want to see from you will help you prioritize which brands to go after and what verticals to focus on. Perhaps they want an offer on a smartphone? Perhaps they are looking for a new computer or high-definition TV? Maybe they want deals on travel and holiday packages, hotels and car rental services? Perhaps they want valuable ticket offerings on sports, leisure and other types of live entertainment, or discounts at some of the finest dining establishments on the planet. Assuming what they want and getting it wrong can result in a lot of time wasted and a lot of energy and focus down the drain. If you don't have offers for products that they do want, then your partnership marketing program will go nowhere fast. It's not enough to market it. Even if you do leverage all the right marketing vehicles and promote the program to customers, you still need the right offers, because offers that aren't relevant or don't have a product that your customer is after will not result in sales traction. Before you embark on your partnership marketing initiatives, it's a good practice to understand what your customers want and to understand if your partner brand's customers want what you are offering before investing in the partnership marketing program.

Distribution Versus the Partner—Sometimes We Can't Get Both!

I recently came across a program where every month a given retailer in my home market is offering their customers an offer in the form of a gift card from another retailer if they spend more during their visit on a given day of the month. If we go back to chapter 3, you will recall that one of the ways by which an organization can grow their business is by increasing average transactional value from existing customers. As a result, in this particular promotion, the retailer is doing just that—if you spend $75 on your visit, they'll give you a $20 gift card from a non-competitive retailer. Interesting marketing partnership and I like how they rotate the offers from month to month, yet one thing came to mind as I examined it further.

The retailer seemed to have partnered with some pretty strong brands for the gift cards, and after researching more, I noticed that they were picking brands with high levels of distribution from coast to coast. Basically, they partner with brands that have a strong national presence and a footprint in every major market across the country. Good strategy, but in doing so, they appeared to have a slight disconnect within another key factor or criterion that would appear to be important for the success of the partnership. The retailer's primary target audience is middle income females who live in major urban centers with a like for quality products, who don't mind spending a little more to obtain more perceived value from their purchase and who like the feeling of a higher-end shopping environment. The partner program disconnect that I am speaking of came in the form of profiling the partner brand.

One gift card brand was that of a quick-service restaurant that targets a low- to mid-end mass public and would be better aligned with a brand that primarily targets male consumers. They have competitors, so when I analyzed it further, I saw that there certainly could have been other options, and I am not sure why the retailer chose to partner with that brand—it could be as simple as other brands not wanting to partner. From a business perspective and strictly looking at it from the retailer's point of view, I came to the conclusion that they likely partnered with that brand during this particular month because of their wide-scale distribution and not their profiling. Sure, other brands might have profiles that more closely matched, but did they have the distribution and retail footprint to make it easy for customers to redeem their gift cards? From what I could tell, they did not.

At that point, it becomes a strategic decision—do we offer a gift card from a brand that may detract from ours somewhat, but has very strong distribution and can fulfill the promise to all customers, or do we not take that risk with our customers and go with a brand that might have less distribution but an offering that is more appealing to our primary customer? Ideally, you want both distribution and a strong profile match to your customers, but in this case the retailer opted for distribution over profile fit given that they could not obtain both in the partnership. It seems like they wanted national coverage and that that was a more important criterion for them.

* * *

In this chapter we discussed associating your brand and the criteria that you want in your partner brand to make you successful in your partnership marketing efforts with them. The next chapter will demonstrate how to put partnership marketing into play for your business once you have chosen the right partner brands.

6

Putting Partnership Marketing into Play

BEST-SELLING AUTHOR STEPHEN Covey states in his book called *The Seven Habits of Highly Effective People* that "People can't live with change if there's not a changeless core inside them. The key to the ability to change is a changeless sense of who you are, what you are about, and what you value." As discussed in chapter 4, there are different kinds of people, and just like people, there are different kinds of partner brands. Some are open to change like teaming up with partner brands to carry out partnership marketing initiatives, while others don't see the value in fusing their marketing efforts with other brands and they know or have decided that it's not for them. That's OK. There is more than one way to sell and market a product or service, and the reality is that if partnership marketing is not recognized throughout the organization as something that is an important strategy and practice and a high strategic priority, then as much as you may want to leverage partnership marketing, you may have some trouble putting it into play.

Some brands are partner-friendly, using different types of marketing partnerships to meet their goals and objectives from distribution to added-value to loyalty programs, while other brands tend to go it alone and only market their products and services directly. Before you put partnership marketing into play within your organization, we need to overview the DNA of partner-friendly brands from a partnership marketing perspective and look at how those brands are leveraging their assets to generate revenue, brand awareness and increased customer loyalty.

PARTNER-FRIENDLY BRANDS

We are talking about partner-friendly brands in the context of partnership marketing. As there are many types of partnerships encompassing a brand's business, it's important to distinguish the collaborative efforts that enhance, supplement and support the brand in its efforts to satisfy the needs and wants of customers by way of their products and services, and to cultivate the partnership marketing relationships that help you do it. Some companies will view their partnership marketing activities as formal ones that involve a high degree of servicing and management, while others will view them as informal laissez-faire affiliations that typically run themselves and don't have a contractual agreement attached to them with standards, guidelines and obligations that the partner brands must adhere to. Either way, it's up to you to govern your partnership marketing initiatives as you like, but my experience has told me that the more formal and well-crafted relationships typically yield better results as they have not only received a higher degree of investment from both brands, but they are highly collaborative and creative and explore the full potential of partnership marketing.

Examples
Coca-Cola

Coca-Cola, the world's largest beverage company, has partnership marketing in their DNA. Since the late 1800's, they have had franchised distribution partnerships with local bottlers in various markets who have exclusivity over a certain territory and have been producing and selling Coca-Cola products for well over one hundred years.

From a partnership marketing perspective, Coca-Cola has always been associated and affiliated with a host of leading partner brands. It was Robert Woodruff, the company's CEO from 1923 to 1954, whose vision it was to associate Coca-Cola with everything that was a major event and leverage the reach to put the brand everywhere and anywhere that customers could enjoy it. Over the years, Coca-Cola has developed sponsorship affiliations and distribution partnerships with World War II, the Olympic Games, Santa Claus and Christmas, The Beatles, McDonald's and the tradition carried on with the FIFA 2010 World Cup.

Coca-Cola is a partner-friendly brand with partnering at the core of their growth strategy, and over time they have leveraged technology, customers, their brand and countless resources to partner with other world-class brands to transform their brand and stay current and 'on top' for generations to come.

Ubisoft

Ubisoft, one of the leading gaming companies on the planet, works with brands to incorporate their products or services into their videogames. This is known as their product placement program. They have worked with brands like Nokia, where characters in their games use Nokia cell phones, so it's part of their actual attire. Ubisoft has also worked with VISA on placement in the popular TV series videogame CSI, where VISA is the brand of credit card used as evidence being examined by characters in the game. Lucile Bousquet of Ubisoft further comments that "because our games can take up to two years to develop, it's the type of opportunity that the partner brand needs to get involved with early on so that they are part of the games' storyline." Secondly, "we offer advertising opportunities to our partner brands where banners, TV commercials, screen savers and other content is embedded into the game. We can also sell in-game advertising where billboards are featured on the streets of outdoor scenes. The benefit of these opportunities is that they don't have to be planned out as far in advance."

Another opportunity is the Ubisoft bundling program, where Ubisoft adds value to an existing brand by providing them with a game that they can bundle into a product. Fast-moving consumer products like breakfast cereals, for example, can feature a free Ubisoft video game CD on the packaging of the box. The brands use these unique opportunities to increase sales and leverage an offer that their competitors will not have. Furthermore, the perceived value for the consumer is about $50, whereas the cost for the partner brand is less than $2 for a PC game (this varies depending on quantities and applicable licenses).

The last opportunity that Bousquet speaks of is that "Ubisoft offers manufacturers opportunities to license our assets by creating T-shirts, toys and other unique items. Because 'gamers' are very loyal to their favorite brand of game, they want products that reflect their favorite video game. It's about giving them what they want." Bousquet confirms that the aforementioned programs have a huge impact on Ubisoft's business. "With over seventy percent of males in North America aged 18 to 24 playing video games and eighty-one percent of households containing at least one PC, our games offer partner brands a unique opportunity to create more awareness with their target audiences and increase sales traction for their products and services. We have games that target kids, tweens, teens and adults, and as a result, we can offer many alternatives, depending on the partner brand's customer profile and who they are targeting."

Google

Brands like Google distribute their search results across several platforms and they partner with brands beyond those that drive people to the Google website or to purchase a Google-powered smartphone to use with their popular search engine. Many of the smartphones from leading manufacturers come equipped with Google applications and many websites use Google Search as their default search engine. Google relies on partners to drive traffic to their popular search engine and, in fact, it's a big part of their user-acquisition strategy, and has been for years.

As more partner brands leverage the power of Google Search as part of their offering to their users or customers, it increases Google's ability to display both what they refer to as natural or organic search results and paid search results (results from those who advertise on Google) to larger audiences, which in turn drives more revenue for Google and their network of partners.

Google does not do much advertising for their brand. If they have done any in recent years, it's very little, and the majority of the ads that I have seen have been targeted to advertisers who may want to advertise on Google as opposed to potential users of their search engine or other products. Google has built their brand by being available where users will want to do an Internet search and are now looking to monetize their other products in the same way.

According to the 2009 BrandZ report by Millward Brown, Google was the top brand once again:

Top 100 Most Valuable Global Brands 2009		
Rank	Brand	Brand Value 2009 ($M)
1	Google	100,039
2	Microsoft	76,249
3	Coca-Cola	67,625
4	IBM	66,622
5	McDonald's	66,575
6	Apple	63,113
7	China Mobile	61,283
8	General Electric	59,793
9	Vodafone	53,727
10	Marlboro	49,460

Google is much more than an Internet search engine or online media property: It's a verb ("I Googled it") and, in some cases, people think that Google is the gateway to the online and digital worlds. With Google having more daily Internet searches than any other Internet property on the planet, they're the kings of the second-most frequented online application on the Internet—searching the Web.

Google is a top search engine and nowadays does more than Web search. It can map out your travel route to visit your brother who lives in Chicago. It can provide you with up-to-the-minute news on the happenings around the globe. It can allow you, via Google Earth, to physically see the destination where you are meeting your friends for lunch, and it can locate, via Google Latitude and your HTC (partner brand) phone, your friends in real time.

Google is a search engine and more, but what are they really good at and why are they so successful at generating high levels of usage for their products? Well, they make good products, that's a given, but what Google also does is make those products available to partners who want to make them available to their users and customers. Google allows their partners a quick and turnkey solution to generating revenue from partnering with them. Many online businesses drive their traffic purely from their relationship with Google, whether it's an informal or formal one. Furthermore, Google makes it easy for partner sites to generate revenue through programs like Google 'AdSense for Content,' which is a program that allows website owners to display targeted Google ads on their website so they can earn revenue from the clicks on impressions of those ads that are made by the users of the website.

Google is great at monetizing or 'making money' from its users by leveraging the power of distribution partnerships. Google has figured out a way to make lots of money online and they have essentially mastered this using the power of partnership marketing. Google knew that if they really wanted to be where they are today, then they had to do more than simply have a great product. They needed to get the product out there and in front of people. They needed to expand their reach and make Google the public's Web search engine of choice. They needed to become the default search engine on most software applications, websites or basically anywhere that someone might want to do a Web search. They needed to be where the users were and follow them wherever they would go.

Google needed to get those paid search results from their advertisers out there and that they did, and much of their success has to do with the distribution partnerships that Google has created over the years with Google 'AdSense for Publishers' and other websites that want to promote Google search results on their site. Revenue is generated by searches and clicks and click-throughs. More searches and more click-throughs mean more revenue for Google and their partners. Google is even the default search engine on various toolbars that are either already part of your Web browser or can be added on to your browser. Google ensures that, wherever someone might want to use a search engine, they have made an attempt to be there. Google understands Internet users, their behavior and where they might want to search the Web. They have created a revenue model around their business that supports and supplements millions and millions of online businesses around the globe and allows for online entrepreneurs not only to leverage the power of Google to be found but also to monetize users by using Google, once they are on your website.

According to Evan Carmichael of evancarmichael.com, "Most people find our website through Google." Carmichael admits that it was not always the case. "As the site grew and more and more users visited us and we increased our page views and unique visitors, Google would periodically contact me to find out if I needed any more information on their products and services. They took notice of what we were doing and would send us 'Google gear' like mouse pads, T-shirts and other stuff and I guess it was that we had started to become a destination site for entrepreneurs and our online ranking started to climb higher as the months went by. Earlier this year, we were invited to their office for a 'Google day' event where website owners could discuss opportunities with product and program managers from Google, and they brought us together to tell our stories and collaborate and speak about how we use Google and what Google can do for us in other ways."

In January 2010, Google contacted Carmichael once again to find out more about his website and to do a review of the ways that he was using Google. They wanted to know whether he was aware of some of Google's new products and to learn about his business and how Google could continue to help him grow his business. This has been helpful to Carmichael and he is now working with Google directly on improving his usage of their products and benefiting from better ad placements and rankings within the search engine results. According to Carmichael, "It's nice to be on their radar and to have opportunities to learn from other Google businesses and the people at Google about how we can do more with them to grow our business."

evancarmichael.com is now one of the top websites in North America for entrepreneurs and continues to prosper from its affiliation and partnership with Google.

The truth is that not everyone is going to be Google or even close to Google, but if you are looking for an example of how a given company has monetized their users or 'visitors' and has essentially made billions of dollars without selling or advertising a single product, it's Google. Google has leveraged distribution marketing partnerships to a very high degree and that's what has given their competition such a hard time in catching up.

When I was in university, one of my marketing professors once told me that the product is the most important factor in determining the success of a brand. That can be argued over and over again, and I am all for strong products. The issue at hand is that it's still up for debate as to whether or not Google is the best Internet search engine on the planet—what is not up for debate is whether they are the most popular and highly recognizable Web search engine. Yes, they have strong products, but what Google really has is a superior business model with distribution marketing and advertising partnerships that fuel it. I am not an expert in the accuracy of search results or how many should be delivered for a given query or how fast a Web search engine should even deliver them. The question is, does it really matter? What Google has is a 'good enough' or 'above average' product, and if not the best, they certainly have the best distribution network, and the perceived value or 'Google factor' as a partner is priceless.

In April 2009, Google announced a partnership with Universal Music for a new music video site called VEVO. According to an article posted on Cnet.com on April 9, 2010, "The move means that Universal Music now has a standalone music video service of its own with higher quality video than what YouTube is offering and they have the right partner in Google to make VEVO a success."

Google is one of the most important companies in the world and is building on the type of collaboration described in the above example. By collaborating in so many ways, from creating a certification program for

Google 'AdWords' that allows search engine marketing professionals to offer their clients a Google-approved service to help them advertise in Google, to allowing websites to use Google Search within their site, to the placement of Google content ads through the 'AdSense for Content' program, Google is really working both formally and informally with their partners to help them grow their businesses and generate revenue from their partnerships. Google continues to be the default search engine on many smartphones, Internet toolbars, websites and other places where people 'search.' Google is globally reaching many people in many languages and continues to be available throughout the world. You need to ask yourself only one question: What would my online business look like today if I was not collaborating or partnering with Google either formally or informally in some way? I think most of you know the answer to that.

Netflix

Other partner-friendly brands, like Netflix (an online entertainment company), have partnered with Microsoft's Xbox 360, Sony's PlayStation 3 and TiVo, to name a few. Basically, Netflix customers who own the aforementioned consoles can stream movie titles from Netflix right into their homes. They have also partnered with Toshiba, Panasonic, Sharp, Sanyo and others where their Blu-ray players and network-connected TVs will be able to stream movies from Netflix. The company has found a way to partner with these brands and transform their business as a result. After all, what good is making thousands of streaming video titles available if you can't get them to viewers?

Netflix started out as an online service that offered flat-rate DVD and Blu-ray Disc rentals by mail, but they realized that in order to stay relevant to the consumer and changing technologies they needed to partner with TV manufacturers and consoles to continue transforming their business and brand value proposition. As consumers shift to the latest technological advances to enjoy their favorite entertainment, it's crucial that companies partner with the category brand leaders who are heading up that transition.

Travel and Accommodation Partners

Some industries have partnership marketing at the core of their DNA. The companies and brands that operate within industries like travel, for example, are more than partner-friendly. They leverage partnership marketing to drive their value proposition, and without their partner brands, they likely wouldn't be in business at all. Online travel sites like Expedia and Travelocity allow users to search for flights, hotels and other travel products from a whole host of partner brands like major hotel chains, independent hotel operators, airlines and car rental companies, and they offer the user an opportunity to view many options before choosing which flight, hotel or car they would like to rent while on holiday. Other sites like Hotwire have partnered with various hotel operators to sell accommodations for them at highly discounted prices in the event that they have excess inventories (rooms) that they want to fill up, and Hotwire makes those rooms available to their users by describing the hotel, its star rating and features, but doesn't release the hotel name until the room is reserved. This way, the hotel operators can target consumers who are price driven and not loyal to any particular hotel brand.

WHAT DOES IT TAKE TO BE PARTNER-FRIENDLY?

It's one thing to establish a partnership marketing relationship, but it's a whole other thing to develop that relationship. Developing your partnership marketing relationship requires a lot of work and a philosophy of wanting your partner brand to succeed just as much as you want your business to succeed. It requires that you have a high degree of openness, transparency and honesty about your business and where you want to take it. What are your key strategies, plans and future endeavors, and how can you and your partner brand best support each other beyond what you are doing currently? Being honest about what the partnership is or isn't doing for your business, so that you can repair it and move forward on a better path, is absolutely required. If you can't be honest with your partner brand, then what will likely happen is that the marketing partnership will continue not to perform properly and the resources that have been put towards it will have gone to waste.

When prospecting for partner brands, as discussed in chapter 4, look for a partner-friendly personality. Is the brand somewhat partner-friendly? Are they not partner-friendly at all or are they very partner-friendly? Will they regard your brand and value proposition as something that can help them in their business and can they help you in turn? Or will they look at you as a potential threat or someone who cannot add value to their business? Once you are ready to put partnership marketing into play, here is a checklist you can use to evaluate prospective partner brands:

❑ **Facts**

Get the facts! What do you know about your prospective partner brand's business and do you know just as much about their business as you do about your own or the business you are working for? Some people think facts are overrated and are not all that necessary, but that's not the case. It's important to understand the facts about a partner brand's business, and you need to make a valiant effort to gain as much information as possible before engaging in a marketing partnership with them. Facts include things like yearly sales, number of customers, number of products, whether they are on trend within their industry and what they have done to grow their business. The more facts you have, the better off you will be in determining how partner-friendly they are.

❑ **Business Strategy**

If you and your prospective partner brand's strategic business plans and goals are not fully aligned, you will not be able to integrate your brands and partner together for success. The value proposition of your brand to theirs and their brand to yours must be clear, apparent and obvious, and it needs to fit in with the overall strategy for the partner brand and to make sense from a financial, logistical and marketing standpoint. It has to leverage the prospective partner brand's existing capabilities, core competencies and everything else that they already do well, and it should support and supplement their existing and future marketing plans and activities. If it doesn't, then your opening conversation with them will come to a pretty quick close.

(continued)

❑ **Buy-In**

You will need strong commitment from senior management and all key levels of the partner brand (once you have that commitment within your own organization; obviously, if you are the business owner, then you need to get buy-in from your staff) to carry out the partnership marketing programs that you are looking to do. Without it, you are wasting your time. You may set off to explore opportunities and even go a fair bit down the road with a partner brand in hopes that you can achieve a marketing partnership with them. All of that will come to an abrupt and quick end if senior management or the owners of the business are not behind it. The last thing you want to do is put in all the work and then have to walk away at the last minute because someone senior in the organization doesn't want to do the deal. Get the buy-in!

❑ **Branding**

In chapter 5 we addressed the concept of associating your brand, yet I can't reiterate this point enough. It's extremely crucial when prospecting for partner brands. You may not need to be with the category leader or the most obvious brands that come to mind when looking at your prospective market for partnerships, but you will want to align and affiliate with a strong brand with the right positioning. You want to work with a brand that is known for having high standards for servicing customers and is well respected in its industry or market sector. Partnering with a brand whose positioning drifts from who you are and doesn't align well will not only create a disconnect in the message to the end customer, it could damage your chances to partner with other brands that could have been the better fit for your brand.

❑ **Customers**

It's necessary that your marketing partnership delivers benefits that neither organization can deliver alone. Some brands will be looking primarily for visibility and awareness; for others, it's about generating sales revenue from the marketing partnership. Either way, without customers or the brands' abilities to reach and connect with them, it's all for nothing. Simply put, if a brand is not willing to promote you to their customers, then they are not partner-friendly and you shouldn't waste your time continuing to discuss opportunities for partnership with them.

❏ Resources

When prospecting your partner brands and opening up your first conversation with them, be sure to get a feel for their resources, whether it be in the form of human capital or otherwise. Your marketing partnership will ultimately be characterized by a commitment from the partner brands to deliver on requirements and obligations, so if you are not confident in the partner brand's commitment to make key resources available to run or manage the relationship, then take it as a sign of bad things to come. Ask the partner brand how their teams are aligned, how many people they have in their marketing department and who could 'physically' do the work to manage the relationship—and whether those people have the necessary skills to pull it off. Who is going to put the calendar of activities together; who will ensure that marketing messaging, creative and vehicles are assembled in a timely manner; and who is going to pull together reports to analyze performance and plan for the future? Ensure that your partner brand is willing to make the necessary resources available. In some cases, like in more informal types of partnerships, you may not require a full-time person to run the partnership marketing program, but in others it may require several people, so be sure of that commitment before going too far down your prospecting and negotiation path.

❏ Targets

Launching a marketing partnership program without setting some clear and concise targets is not a good way to put things into play, as you will encounter difficulty down the line in determining if the marketing partnership is meeting your requirements. Decide your key performance indicators (KPIs) in advance, set targets for customers acquired and revenue generated, and ensure that you are targeting partner brands that can deliver and help you meet your targets. KPIs will be different for every business.

Set a number for customers that you wish to acquire through your partnership marketing program so that you choose marketing partners

(continued)

that will positively contribute to your target. It's not a bad idea to communicate those targets to your partner brand or even ask them how many of their customers they think they can acquire for you. Ask them how many customers they will communicate your offer to and what their typical response rates are for such a program. Or, once you find out more about their business, you can apply response rates and conversion metrics from similar programs to the program you are looking to do with them.

❑ **Stability**
As with any program, you are making an investment when you create a marketing partnership with a partner brand. You will invest time, resources and money towards something that is meant to yield positive results and a good return on investment. One of the biggest mistakes that organizations make is to partner with brands that are not in a stable cash position or not stable overall. Partnering with a brand that is going through a major downsizing effort or reorganization, is in the process of being acquired or is changing their brand and product strategy altogether is likely not a good way to go. Partnering with businesses that are stable, that will be around and that are in a 'good place' from a business standpoint is ideal. Not only will they have the ability to focus on the marketing partnership and to work together to yield some positive results from the investment they have made, they will also be around as a business to carry out the partnership. Partner with brands that are stable, not ones that are in flux and may not be around next month.

❑ **Openness**
You should be looking for partner brands that are open with their business strategy—brands that are open in their communication related to anything from potential areas of competition between your brand and theirs to their customer acquisition strategies and how they market their products. Without openness, you can't properly identify opportunities and potential threats as partners and you can't explore the full potential for your marketing partnership. Being open is more than just discussing one particular tactic they use or sharing some data on where their industry is heading. It's about providing you with everything you need to know from a marketing perspective to understand what can be leveraged to

help you meet your targets for the partnership. You can't increase your chances for success from a program without knowing about your partner brand. If they are not open and not making themselves available in terms of their product development plans, market and customer acquisition strategies, strategic direction and how valuable their business really is, you don't stand a chance of being able to develop the relationship beyond establishing it in the first place.

❑ **Technology**

Does the partner brand have the software and other technologies to carry out what you are looking for them to do? If they don't, can it be integrated quickly without becoming a major cost? Do they need to adapt existing systems and are they easily able to communicate your marketing partnership to their internal workforce and throughout their organization? Can they easily train their franchise partners or call center or sales force on the new component of your partnership? Technology is important and needs to be looked at from all angles—from what it will take to communicate the marketing partnership to the target audience to tracking orders, redeeming offers and paying revenue share to partners. Making tools and templates available to partners in an easy fashion and supporting partners in any way possible all relies on technology. You need to invest in technology, but be reminded that your investment should produce a nice return, so if you are going to develop software or license it to run your programs or incur in-house development fees, you need to account for that when looking at opportunities with partner brands. You may want to work with brands that are more nimble and can easily deploy technology without you having to bear the brunt of any incremental costs.

To assess the information, you will need to have preliminary discussions with the potential partner. Much can be said for how they interact during those first few meetings—if they are 'partner-friendly' and warm to your proposition. It's a good idea to do your own research on their company. Visit their websites, download their apps, become a friend on their social media pages and go to their store locations. Engage with them and even go through the process of becoming one of their customers; by doing so, you can determine how they engage and interact with customers and get some valuable insight and facts about the way they do business. Who knows . . . you might even learn more about the partner brand than some of the people working there! Find out as much as you can about how they run their business and what they do to be successful. Doing so will help you reach an opinion about whether they are the right partner brand for you.

It's hard to tell which brands are partner-friendly at an initial glance when you haven't had any experience working with them in the past. The reality is that you can't know for sure, and it's the fear of the unknown that deters marketers from putting partnership marketing into play. There is a loss of control in working with another brand. It's up to you to determine your evaluation criteria and use the aforementioned list as a guideline in your unique situation. If you are developing more informal types of marketing partnerships, then you will likely require fewer criteria in making your decision.

WORK WITH ABLE AND WILLING PARTNER BRANDS

Some brands are going to be extremely partner-friendly in some aspects of their business, but maybe not in others. One of my clients was looking to run a 'gift with purchase' program where customers would receive an iPod Nano with the purchase of my client's products. When I called Apple to discuss this opportunity, they told me to go to their store and buy the iPods directly. That wasn't exactly the response I was looking for, or expecting at the time. I'd seen Apple partner before, as in the case of a program with their iTunes property and Starbucks coffee outlets. As my client has a strong brand themselves, I figured Apple would at least want to hear the details of the partnership program. Well, they didn't, which is fine. However, the lesson learned, which I am passing on in this book, is that you cannot chase down partner brands that don't want to partner.

You need to ensure that you are working with brands that will want to support your goals and objectives for the marketing partnership, not just create a transactional relationship. Some brands don't want to discount products or be perceived to be giving away something for free, even if they get massive amounts of exposure from a partner brand. Sometimes it has nothing to do with the program or partner brand. Rather, it is simply a case of it not being part of their strategy. Apple does partner on other fronts and uses best-in-class content providers like Google and YouTube in their new iPad, for example. Maybe partnering to give away the already popular iPod Nano just isn't part of their strategy.

Now that you know how to identify a partner-friendly brand, it's time to put partnership marketing into play. Remember the old saying, "fail to plan and you can plan to fail." We discussed the different types of partnerships, the importance of ECP when looking at partner prospects, how you can leverage the power of partnership marketing to drive revenue for your business and how to correctly associate your brand. Now let's talk about you, your brand and your partnership marketing program.

- What are you going to do to use partnership marketing in your business?
- How are you going to collaborate with partner brands and leverage their assets and competencies to meet your objectives?

The first stage in answering those questions is to formulate the 4 Ps to successful marketing partnerships.

THE 4 PS TO SUCCESSFUL MARKETING PARTNERSHIPS

PLAN for Success

The first P is 'plan for success.' You can only do that if you have identified your objectives for your partnership marketing program. Consider these questions:

- What do you intend to achieve from your marketing partnerships? List the end results or goals with a finite projected timeline for when you are going to achieve them. For example, you may have a combination of shorter-term goals, like launching a few short-term tactical promotional programs to increase brand awareness, followed by some longer-term goals to leverage marketing partnerships to engage in co-marketing a whole new product by the end of the year. Success is not guaranteed by any stretch no matter what type of marketing programs you are using to grow your business, but you can certainly increase your chances for success if you plan for it.

- What type of marketing partnerships will you use and why will they be attractive to prospective brands?
- How many partner brands do you need?
- Can you prospect brands in certain verticals or is it better to go horizontal?

Those questions need to be answered to effectively plan for success. This is a good place to list your strategies to grow market share, increase profit, build brand awareness, retain clients, cross-sell and up-sell new products and services, penetrate international markets, etc. What are your targets, assumptions, forecasts and estimates for the upcoming year?

PROFILE Your Brand

You need to assign a characterization to your brand. I am not speaking of a mission statement or a company history or vision for the future, but an account of what your brand stands for, your core values as a company, and what is unique and can be distinguished about your products and services. Furthermore, this may include your brand values or positioning in your market and how you provide solutions to satisfy the needs and wants of customers.

There are three generally accepted methods for measuring the value of a brand, which I picked up when I was working at AOL:

1. The **cost method** refers to valuing the brand based on costs incurred to build it up since launch. This method does not take into account the revenue-generating potential of a brand but rather what's been spent to get it to where it is.

2. The **income method** measures the net present value of the brand and its ability to generate positive future earnings and cash flows. Branded products can sell for higher prices and benefit from better economies of scale than non-branded items.

3. The **market method** involves gathering data on market transactions for similar brands in the same category and comparing them to assign a value known as a 'royalty rate.' Typically, the royalty rate is defined as the market rate derived from licensing or royalty agreements for similar assets. This is easier said than done, because all brands are different and direct comparisons are hard to make. Generally you need to adjust the royalty rate because the analysis has to reflect the differences in the brands that are being compared.

If you are looking to align your brands to those that have a similar value, be sure that you are calculating the value by using the same method that the partner brand is using in order to be sure it's like to like. Brand value is an important metric, but only for very large brands. Smaller businesses that don't spend a lot of money on branding, have not been around for long and have limited awareness as compared to larger brands should not focus on their brand as an asset to be leveraged in a marketing partnership. Instead, they should focus on their products, value proposition, abilities to share revenue and willingness to be nimble, creative, and easy to work with, and their speed in execution by not having to cut through piles of red tape.

Are you a behavioral brand—such as 1-800-GOT JUNK?, the people you call when you're cleaning out after moving or renovating, but certainly not every day or week or month—or do you appeal to people with certain demographics, or both? What do your customers look like? If you are behavioral, then your customers buy your products for certain occasions or uses or are looking for certain product benefits to help them with a problem that needs solving. If you are selling to an audience that is of a certain age, gender or income, lives in a certain location and is at a certain life stage, then you are more of a brand that appeals to certain demographics. Perhaps you are both? Maybe you are one for certain products and another for other products. Either way, it's about developing a brand profile or 'description' for your target audience (which should resemble your best customers) and including the relevant demographic and behavioral information such as buying patterns and other characteristics. Finally, be sure to list how many customers you have for each type of product or projected sales for those products or customers to be acquired for the year ahead.

The brand profile is also where you want to include the marketing assets that you will want to leverage in the partnership—which we overviewed in chapter 2.

PRODUCE Your Partner Brand Criteria

Your partner brand criteria are the standards by which a partner can be judged and they can help you pick the right partners for you. Essentially, it's about listing what you are looking for in associating with a partner brand as referred to in chapter 5. You can choose your own criteria based on how formal or informal you want your partnership marketing program to be. Some of the more popular ones are size of opportunity, relevance to your business, geography, mutuality and growth potential. The rest are listed in more detail in chapter 5. The key is to assign a level of importance to each partner brand criterion and put them in a scorecard. The more important criteria will have higher scores associated with them, while less important ones are assigned lower scores. Once you have your prospective partner brand criteria (listed below) together, you will be able to check off on the scorecard whether or not the brand has each criterion. If they have the criterion, they get the full score; if they don't, they get the same amount but as a negative score. If it's not an applicable criterion, then the partner brand gets no score. Here is an example for a software company that is looking to partner with partner brands in the dental vertical.

Sample Prospective Partner Brand Criteria

Rank	Measurement/Criterion	Yes	No	N/A	Y	N	Score
1	The brand is widely recognized within the industry				5	−5	0
2	The brand is widely recognized on a national level				5	−5	0
3	The brand has a strong reach to the primary target market (dentists)				4	−4	0
4	The brand has a strong presence in prominent geographic areas				4	−4	0

(continued)

Rank	Measurement/Criterion	Yes	No	N/A	Y	N	Score
5	The brand enhances our proposition to the primary target market (dentists)				3	−3	0
6	The brand is a clear leader in its respective category (media, distribution, etc.)				3	−3	0
7	The brand is relevant to the business of dentistry (sells to dentists)				2	−2	0
8	The brand has a head office in the United States				2	−2	0
9	The brand uses the right vehicles and channels to promote our proposition				1	−1	0
10	The brand has an online component to their business and it's a focus for their business				1	−1	0

Great prospects will have a score between 23 and 30
Good prospects will have a score between 15 and 22
Average prospects will have a score between 8 and 14
Poor prospects will have a score between −30 and 7

PREPARE Your Tools

You can't develop your marketing partnerships without the tools that will allow you to establish the right relationships.

Partnership Application Form

The purpose of the partnership application form is for you to evaluate any incoming requests for partnership to see if the brands are a good fit for your business. You may have identified certain brands for partnership and be going after them in your outgoing efforts, but you need a process to profile incoming requests as they approach you and your company for partnership. Below is a sample form and some data you may want to collect to help you evaluate the partner prospects.

A Sample Partnership Application Form

Purpose
Thank you for your interest in becoming an authorized partner. Please fill out the application form below. We will follow up with you after we review your application.

I am a:

❏ Publisher   ❏ Business consultant   ❏ Sales agent

Publishers
Business magazines, e-Learning, professional journals and management publications
Business consultants
Service design, systems and processes, resource planning and practice management
Sales agents
Financial, accounting, legal, insurance and business services or products

Partnership Application Form
Company Contact Information

Company Name:

Address: City:

State/Prov: ZIP/Postal code: Country:

Tel: Fax: Email:

Years in Business: Total Revenues for Previous Year:

Employees: # Offices: # Salespeople:

Industry/Industries Serviced: # Customers:

Geographic Areas Serviced: _____   Public or Privately Owned:

Average Annual Revenue: ❏ $0–$10M   ❏ $10M–$50M   ❏ >$50M

Competition

List your top four competitors, by geographic area and product line:

1.
2.
3.
4.

Familiarity with Our Products

How long have you been familiar with our products?

❏ 0–2 years   ❏ 2–5 years   ❏ 5+ years

What other products do you currently carry?

1.
2.
3.
4.

What other qualifications do you have that will enable you to sell our products?

Answer:

How do you intend to market our products to your potential and existing customer base?

Answer:

(*continued*)

Sales Estimates

Please provide your best estimate for the number of customers you expect to sell our solution to per year:

Year 1:
Year 2:
Year 3:

Consent

I hereby consent to the verification of any or all of the information above:

Company:

Title:

_____   _____

Name of Applicant   Date

Partner Development Pipeline

A simple spreadsheet can work just as well as any software program to track the progress of your partner prospects and where you are with them. You can include fields as follows:

- Name of target company (prospective partner brand name)
- Interest level (prospect partner brand is very, somewhat or mildly interested in opportunity)
- Contact name and details (name, title, phone number and email for the person you are dealing with)
- Partnership marketing program (the type of program: e.g., added value, distribution, reseller, sponsorship)
- Stage (where you are with the prospect: prospecting, pitch presentation, negotiation, working towards closure)
- Customers (how many customers do they have and how many will they market to)

- Date pitched (when did you first contact them and send them your pitch)
- Notes (any additional information about next steps for your discussions, etc.)
- Company lead (who in your company is leading the discussion, as it may be someone other than you)

Partner Pitch Deck

The partner pitch deck is your presentation to the prospective partner brand. It's the hook that you need to garner their interest and lead you from prospecting to negotiation and establishing a marketing partnership. You can use many different formats to put together your pitch, with Microsoft PowerPoint being the most typical. Your pitch deck should contain the following slides:

- An updated profile for your brand
- A positioning statement
- Facts about the partner brand and how they relate to your brand
- Why you are getting in touch with them
- Details about your products and services
- The opportunity
- The details of which partner brand will be doing what
- Summary

If you would like to receive a sample partner pitch deck, just send me an email at ron@geysermarketing.com and put 'Partner Pitch Deck' in the subject line and I will send you one.

Partner Snapshot

The partner snapshot is a tool that you use to evaluate the opportunity with the prospective partner brand internally to decide whether you are ready to go forward with a partner agreement. The snapshot should give the management of your company details on the partner brand and an overview of the key deal terms being discussed. The partner snapshot should contain:

- Key contact information for your partner brand
- Deal overview and rationale for creating the marketing partnership (include opportunities, costs, forecasted revenue, critical timelines and marketing value)
- Marketing commitments and obligations from both brands
- Rationale and expectations
- Background (partner overview)
- Key risks (in doing the deal and not doing the deal)
- Sign-offs (CEO, Operations, IT, Marketing Services, etc.)

Partner Agreement

I have a saying: Always sign a partner agreement with a company that you trust and want to partner with—never sign one with a company that you don't trust and do not want to partner with.

You might think it's a pretty logical next step, but you would be surprised how many companies launch their marketing partnership without even a simple term sheet, let alone a partnership marketing agreement.

Elements of a Partnership Marketing Agreement

1. Define the marketing partnership:
   What is this marketing partnership about and what does it mean to be partners?

2. Obligations:
   What does each company have to do and what are they responsible for in the partnership? What have you negotiated? This includes everything from lead-generating activities to the products that are being promoted and the standards by which they will be promoted. This also may include the frequency with which each party performs each task.

3. Trademarks and branding:
   Which trademarks and cross-licenses and brands have been made available for use? How should they be used and where should they be used?

4. Marketing plans:
   A detailed overview of the marketing plan to market the other parties' products and services. Everything from placements to channels being used, media, email marketing and anything else that is relevant.

5. Term:
   How long is the term of the partnership and can the partnership be terminated if necessary? Are we talking about one year? Two years? Be sure to outline a timeline that makes sense and will allow the marketing partnership to flourish, but at the same time will not lock it in too long, should parties want to go their separate ways.

6. Payments:
   How are payments being made? Who is collecting the transactional revenue and who is paying the other partner? What currency is being used to make the payments and what form will they be in? Wire transfer? Check? You need to be specific on payments and collecting revenues. Will they be made monthly? Quarterly?

7. Tracking and reporting:
   Which key metrics apply? What is to be tracked, and what needs to be reported to the other party and how often? Who is tracking what? We're talking about leads, conversions, sales, etc. Think of all the metrics and be sure to outline the commitments or targets. Perhaps you have an exclusive marketing partnership whereby the marketing partner must achieve certain sales targets to keep their exclusivity. Be sure that it's included in there!

Naturally, your partnership marketing agreements should contain all the necessary legal clauses like confidentiality, disclaimers, warranties and liabilities beyond the marketing clauses I have listed above. Be sure to speak

(continued)

to a lawyer about those items and ensure that you are protected. When marketing through a third party, it's important to have an agreement that you can refer back to should any disputes ever arise about the nature of the marketing partnership and what is expected of both sides.

•   •   •

Once you have put these 4 Ps to successful marketing partnerships into play and are getting ready to launch your programs with your partner brand, you will want to be sure to practice smart collaboration with them. I cover that in the next chapter.

7

Practicing Smart Collaboration

WHAT IS SMART COLLABORATION? In the context of partnership marketing, I define it as two or more organizations that

- have engaged in a marketing partnership;
- are using common sense to maximize their opportunities by sharing knowledge;
- are aligned and leveraging the partnership to move forward to meet their respective goals.

Those who practice smart collaboration are working with their partner brands as a collective unit, embracing the marketing obligations that they have to undertake to make their partnership achieve great levels of success for themselves and for their partner brands. They understand that their marketing union fills a gap that they couldn't fill on their own and are committed to bringing whatever valuable elements they can to the relationship to optimize it and make it better than it was before. Brands that follow the principles of smart collaboration and have the framework described below to get the most out of their marketing partnerships realize that partnerships morph over time. Therefore, they will need to change the products, offers, marketing vehicles and technologies to meet the demands of the market, and they must be flexible in embracing those changing dynamics so that their marketing partnership remains relevant and performs at a high level into the future. That is smart collaboration.

Elements of a Partnership Marketing Smart Collaboration Framework

1. Partner referral process
2. Partnership engagement strategy
3. Partner collaboration tools
4. Training

PARTNER REFERRAL PROCESS

The referral process is how the secondary partner brand encourages their customers to engage with the primary partner brand, and how they are ultimately rewarded for doing so. It's different for every type of marketing partnership—you may recall that we discussed the most common types in chapter 1—but the theme is the same all around: You need to develop a referral process that connects to your partner brand's marketing value chain and aligns with their success criteria in order to measure your partnership marketing program and practice smart collaboration.

The partner brand's marketing value chain refers to:

- Their target audience
- Brand objectives—acquisition or retention of customers, new revenue stream, etc.
- Campaign development—where does your proposition fit in?
- Measures—monitoring, KPIs (e.g., customer conversion rates), results (did it meet target?)

Mapping the Partner Brand's Marketing Value Chain

When you are partnering with another brand, you need to understand that their marketing value chain is likely going to be different than yours. The practices that encompass how the partner brand generates customers to buy their products, and which marketing vehicles, advertising messages and pricing models they promote, are key in determining how the marketing partner will refer business to you and vice versa. You need to understand how the marketing partner interacts with their target audience and existing customers to effectively leverage their marketing value chain to support you as best as they can. What is their marketing communications strategy? What is their promotion mix? Which vehicles do they use and which are most effective?

Connecting Your Offering to the Partner Brand's Marketing Value Chain

Now that you have mapped out the partner brand's marketing value chain, you need to connect your offering to the marketing activities that will best support and supplement your brand and offering. It may be as simple as picking and choosing the cheapest or most cost-effective activities, like promotion on a partner brand's website or in their email marketing campaigns, as opposed to having to develop signage and POS materials for their retail operations. Maybe it's more varied and you would like to communicate your offer through multiple vehicles and engage with them online and offline and determine which pulls better. Perhaps your business is an added-value component that is to be cross-promoted with products that are sold through their inbound call center? In any event, whether you are selling to businesses or to consumers, you need to connect to the activities that will yield the best results for your business and for the partner brand without compromising or conflicting with any current initiatives.

Aligning with the Success Criteria of the Partner Brand

What are the key success criteria for the partner brand? You may have an idea of what it means for you to be successful, but a solution that helps the partner brand sell more may not help you. In most cases, partner brands are looking to generate revenue from their partners, so their activities that promote the primary brand need to generate revenue. The question is how much revenue can you generate (as the primary brand) for your secondary partner brand, and is it enough to warrant them undertaking the obligations that you want them to undertake to fulfill their end of the partnership? If you can't generate high levels of sales and revenue for your partner brand, you may need to align with their other success criteria, like helping them increase customer satisfaction, brand reputation and growth into new business categories, for starters. There are different viewpoints out there as to what makes for a successful business, but as highlighted in chapter 4, being economically successful is crucial to the meaningfulness and importance of your marketing partnership. Developing a marketing partnership that doesn't align to at least one criterion for the partner brand's success will result in collaboration, but not smart collaboration.

Metrics

Get your partner brand to agree to how many referrals they are going to generate for you and, if it's vice versa, how many you are going to generate for them. With sponsorship marketing partnerships, it may simply be about visibility and impressions as opposed to tracking referrals for sales activities. Licensing marketing partnerships are not as much based on referrals as they are on generating purchase orders from retailers who will ultimately resell the product. Referrals are difficult to estimate. Use history, be realistic and—I can't stress this enough—get 'buy in' on your metrics so that nobody falls short of expectations and what has been forecasted is in fact doable. Metrics must be achievable and both brands need to agree. Without setting some advanced metrics on what you think you can achieve, it will be hard to determine how successful your marketing partnership has been for you; and without having goals in place, you can't adjust and tweak the program going forward.

Furthermore, when you have a few partners in place, it's important to map out how they compare to each other in terms of referrals to your business. A simple way to do this is to list the referral partners in one column of a spread-sheet alongside a neighboring column titled 'number of referrals' followed by a third column titled 'percentage of referrals,' which is the percentage of the overall referrals that a given partner sends over to you, followed by a column titled 'conversion,' which essentially means the number of referrals that turned into paying customers for your business. Finally, you add a column calculating the 'total number of customers' generated by the partner.

Here is an example:

Partner	Number of Referrals	Percentage of Referrals	Conversion	Total Number of Customers
ABC	1,569	12%	4.0%	63
XYZ	8,467	66%	0.3%	25
GHS	2,863	22%	9.0%	258
Total	12,899	100%		346

In the above example, a partner like XYZ may drive significantly more referrals than partners like ABC and GHS, but when it comes to converting their referrals into actual paying customers they perform quite poorly in comparison, meaning that there could be an issue with the value proposition that you are offering at the end-customer level. This brings us to our partnership engagement strategy.

PARTNERSHIP ENGAGEMENT STRATEGY

Your partner brands will interact with your brand and be 'engaged' based on your ability to offer to them and their customers a value proposition that allows you and your partner brands to leverage what you need from the relationship to drive your marketing partnership forward. Without high levels of partnership engagement, you may be collaborating but you will not be collaborating smartly, because you have not been able to find something of value or of any significance to leverage in the marketing partnership and, therefore, the frequency of interaction between your brand and the partner brand will be low, making your program dormant and of no value to either of the brands.

Establishing the Partner Value Proposition

In general there are five types of benefits that a partner brand will want from a marketing partnership. If you want to keep your partner brand engaged, you need to ensure that you are delivering at least two of them.

1. An opportunity to earn incremental *revenue*
2. An exceptional *product* or *service* to add value to what they are already offering
3. A *brand* that enhances theirs
4. An opportunity to reach your *customers*
5. A unique piece of *content* that you can give them that is not available anywhere else

Revenue

Your partner brand can generate revenue by promoting your product or service to their customers in different ways, depending on what type of product or service you have. The key is to determine how your assets can best serve a partnership. For example, if you are a subscription-based business, then offering a portion of revenue on your recurring revenue stream is an attractive thing to make available in your marketing partnership.

Here are some of the more popular models to generate revenue in a marketing partnership:

- Recurring
  Partner brands like recurring revenue streams, which they get in the form of a portion of the revenue that you are generating from an end customer that they referred to you; they can count on it as stable and predictable. This is commonly used with subscription-based products or services that have regular billing cycles, such as monthly or quarterly.

- Sharing
  Commonly used in distribution marketing partnerships. Your partner brand effectively takes a portion or 'share' of the revenue generated for

selling the product that you will be fulfilling to their customers and remits the balance to you. This is common where the secondary partner brand wants to own the transaction with their customers, but doesn't want the responsibility for product promotion, development and fulfillment to the end customer. This is different than margin- or consignment-based revenue models, which are used in traditional physical distribution or retailing type transactional-based relationships where a retailer will be responsible for warehousing, promoting, delivering and servicing the product from which they generate a margin.

- Bounty
  The bounty revenue model is a form of commission payable as a one-time fee for sending a customer order. This is typically a fixed dollar amount that has been agreed upon by both brands, such as $25 sent from one brand partner to another every time a customer is referred over. It's quite common in cases where one transaction occurs as opposed to several recurring transactions.

- Performance Thresholds
  Thresholds are typically put into place to incentivize the partner brand to continue to market the product over a period of time. This typically occurs with recurring revenue streams that drop in percentage points throughout the lifetime of the customer that was acquired. For example, the partner brand may get five percent per transaction every month that the subscriber pays in year one, but that may drop to three percent in year two. The higher percentage in year one acts as an incentive for the partner brand to continue generating new subscribers for you. Because the secondary partner brand is not all that involved in retaining those customers over time and that responsibility is the primary partner brand's, the percentage drops in subsequent years.

Either one or a combination of the above revenue models can be used to compensate your partner brand or have them compensate you for generating customers for them. One of the things you should consider when thinking about the revenue stream for your partner brand is that the amount of money you have available to send over to your partner brand will be limited, especially if you are giving their end customer a 'special offer' that is eating into your margins. You will still want to make money on the deal, so as there are only so many ways that you can slice the pie, so to speak, you will need to decide how much you are investing in your end-customer offer (which we discuss below) and how much partner revenue you are going to make available. Some partnerships will be more about driving partner revenue, and some will be about creating brand awareness and providing your partner with a special offer for their customers. Depending on what you decide to do with your partner brand, a larger portion of the available revenue may go either to the partner or toward a better offer for the end customer.

Product

Partner brands will only value a product that enhances their proposition. Essentially, the product must give them something that they don't have already. The products or services that you propose to build your partner-brand value proposition around have to be strong. They need to be in demand and have a high perceived-value association, especially to your partner brand's customers. The goal here is to learn about their customers and what they may need or want, and to determine how you fit into that equation. If your product is not relevant, then the partnership will be flawed. Take a generic MP3 player manufacturer that is willing to give sixty percent revenue sharing to a partner brand for every transaction they facilitate. If the partner brand's customers have a tendency to purchase more high-end or branded products like an iPod, they likely will not be able to refer any business. No matter how attractive the revenue stream, it will not amount to much for either partner.

Branding

In the world of branding, big typically likes to work with big, and smaller, lesser-known brands are more likely to engage with smaller, lesser-known partner brands. We see this in cases like NFL.com and their relationship with Ticketmaster for their Ticket Exchange program (the NFL is a leading professional American-style football league and Ticketmaster is a leader in processing, managing and fulfilling tickets for sporting and entertainment events). Although it's quite common, this is not always the case, as some heavily branded companies will want to partner with lesser-known companies if those companies have a product or service that complements their offering and enhances their value proposition to their end customer.

Customers

The final benefit to the partner brand is that of end customers. If you have a customer or target audience profile that resembles the one that they are looking to market to, then you have an opportunity for them. Marketing to your customers by leveraging your assets and adding value to your offering with their products and services will certainly be of interest to partner brands looking to grow their business. It could be as simple as leveraging content for your website where they have more expertise than you do and it's an area that you want to improve and make available to your customers. Furthermore, it could be a distribution opportunity to engage your customer mailing list with a free trial offer that the partner brand will make exclusively available to your customers for a given period of time. (Note that this is different than providing your partner brand with customer data. Most companies will not allow another brand to market to their customers directly, so the way to get around this is to have your partner brand, who already has a relationship with their customers, market your product for you. It's likely to be more successful than marketing directly, as customers tend to pay more attention to offers from partner brands.) Either way, making customers available by leveraging your existing customer marketing activities is a very cost-effective way for partner brands to acquire a new customer.

Content

One of the ways to create some stickiness around your brand is to provide your customers with unique content and an experience they can't get anywhere else. Independent films are often only available for viewing at certain retro-style cinemas before coming out on Blu-ray or DVD. Cable companies will often make episodes of certain TV programs available for online viewing at their website as the only place you can typically see them. Celebrities stop in at certain book stores or chains for meets and greets with fans and to sign personalized copies of their new book. Partner brands are no different. They want unique content from their partners as well. If you can provide online videos, blog posts, podcasts and content for an upcoming whitepaper and make it unique, then the partners will listen up and hold value in that, especially if it's great content and not available anywhere else. We live in a content-rich society with billions upon billions of Internet searches being done every day by people looking for content. Unique and exclusive content from a partner brand can really create some benefits to a brand looking to offer more to their customers, users or members.

Establishing the End Customer Value Proposition

The end customer is the one who will ultimately be buying your product via the partnership marketing program that you are offering to the prospective partner or vice versa. The end customer could be an individual or a business. Establishing your end customer value proposition is just as important as getting a partner value proposition together.

In the case of a sponsorship play, there may not be anything special offered to the partner brand's customers and the partner value proposition is where it takes flight and ends. There may be no end customer value proposition in the case of some distribution partnership programs as well, given that partner brands may choose not to discount or bundle special offers to the other brand's audience, and therefore the product or service being marketed is the same as it is in terms of its availability in direct or other partner channels.

If you are engaged in an affinity and added-value partnership program, then you definitely need to think about your offer to the end customer. If it's not a 'market competitive' or unique offering with something compelling in it for the end customer, then forget about it—you are not going to generate sales traction. You need to have something that will have high perceived value to the end customer.

Your Checklist for Developing the Right End Customer Value Proposition for Your Partners' Customers

❑ How is the offer messaged? Does it have the right wording? Language?
❑ Is your offer compelling? Does it make sense? Is it on the mark?
❑ Does your offer meet everyone's needs?
❑ Does the offer outshine your competitors' offers?
❑ Is your offer economically feasible?

Take a look at history. What has worked in the past? Test different creative pieces and see what pulls best, then use that in your direct marketing activities in your partnership. You might not have the right offer from the start and that's why you need to test your offers and rotate them within your added-value or affinity program. Understand your partners' key timings for business; for example, work with them at the right time of the year if their business is seasonal. Ask your partner about their customers and what they prefer. What do they like and how do they interact with them?

Fit into how your partner communicates with their customers and do the same on your end when adding partners to your partner roster. Have them leverage the best possible vehicles for communication. If they don't get a great response on direct mail and do much better with email marketing to customers because they are an online company, then leverage your email marketing efforts to integrate your partners' offers as well. Customers like to interact with brands in different ways. McDonald's interacts at their counters, not at their websites, Zappos likes to interact online and Dell does a good part of their sales via their call center. Think about the offer and where you are placing it.

Leverage the Marketing Partnership

Leveraging your marketing partnership is all about your ability to influence your partner brand and engage them further in the program. The more important the marketing partnership is to them, the more leverage you will have. If you have a strong partner value proposition and a strong end customer value proposition that is yielding good results, then you will certainly have more negotiating power when it comes to launching new initiatives with your existing partner.

Truly leveraging the relationship means that you are getting fair value and that the program is mutually beneficial to both parties. Partnerships that are well leveraged have significant clout in the business. They have senior management buy-in, so that when more assets are required to take the partnership further, those assets are made available. This is made possible by demonstrating the worthwhile nature of the partnership and the value it is bringing to both organizations. In other words, your ability to leverage your partnership is entirely dependent on the strength of the value propositions that you are bringing to each other.

Metrics

Take a closer look at your partner brands and what you are doing with the ones that are garnering success for your business. Where do they promote your offer, and what have you been able to leverage from them? Identify which actions drive more referrals and convert more. What are the end customers doing when they arrive at your brand? Are they spending time on your website or are they leaving right away? How long do they spend on your site, interacting with your offer, or on the phone if the call to action takes them to your call center? Which products or services are they buying most (if you are offering several of them) and which ones should your partner be promoting based on the most successful partner programs you have had to date? You need to profile each partner brand and what they are doing to refer business back to you.

Here is an example:

Partner	Compelling Offer	Prominent Marketing Vehicle	Frequency	Revenue Model	Brand Fit
ABC	Yes	Email Marketing	Monthly	Bounty	Strong
XYZ	No	Website	Rotating Placement	Bounty	Medium
GHS	Yes	Call Center	Daily	Bounty	Strong

Continuing the earlier example, here are your three partner programs, with some data regarding each one. As cited earlier, partner XYZ drove a significant amount of referrals for the given period (8,467), nearly three times as much as the next partner (GHS), but had a very low conversion of 0.3% compared to the 9% that GHS had. Some of the key things to note is that XYZ did not have a compelling offer during the period. They put forward a standard offer that resembled those being offered in other marketing channels. Furthermore, they used their website to drive referrals, which was thought to be a good idea given their high volumes of website traffic, but somehow the traffic did not convert. Another observation is that, as a brand fit, they were categorized as medium, while the other partner brands had a strong brand fit—they are very relevant and highly aligned to your products and services.

The referral and conversion metrics tell the story of how each partner brand performed, while the profiles of the partners tell the story of why the results were what they were. This gives you the ability to provide feedback to partner XYZ and advise them that maybe they need to promote a different offer to their customers—something more compelling; furthermore, you have more negotiating power to leverage other marketing vehicles beyond the website, given the high performance that vehicles like email marketing and the call center are generating with your other partner brands. Shifting offers, vehicles and the frequency of vehicles could have a positive, negative or neutral impact on your partner programs; regardless, it should be done in situations that require improvement because they are underperforming. Without the metrics for how each partner engages with you and your points of leverage in the relationship, as well as the data on how many customers each is referring to you, it's impossible to work towards optimizing relationships so that they perform better.

PARTNER COLLABORATION TOOLS

Partner collaboration tools relate to the things that help partner brands collaborate, such as software and technologies that you leverage with your partner brand to facilitate the running of your marketing partnership. Given that every partnership is different, the tools that you use may have different applications and functions as needed to support the marketing partnership.

I suggest that before building or buying the tools needed, you test your partnership marketing program and determine what the true market opportunity is. If you see it as being sizable and worth the initial investment to set up a framework for collaboration with your marketing partner, especially one that later can be leveraged with other marketing partners, then it may be worth your while to invest in some already existing tools or create some tools to make managing and communicating with your partner brand that much easier.

Here are some vendors you may want to check out:

1. Salesforce.com—partner relationship management (Chatter)
2. NetSuite—partner relationship management
3. SAP—business partners management

You can expect that your partner brands will want real-time access to certain data regarding the partnership, so be sure to have tools that will allow them to log into a special website on their own to see how many referrals they have given, how many converted and how much revenue they are generating from the partnership. You should be looking for the same from your partner. If that's not possible, just agree that at the end of every month, you will send your partner brand a manually generated report that gives them an overview of the performance of the program.

Some tools can be automated, while others may be manual. By looking at how your marketing partnership is performing, you will be able to determine whether or not you should be investing in creating or purchasing more sophisticated tools beyond basic, manually updated spreadsheets that are mailed out once a month. The key is to match the tools to the performance of the partnership.

Collaboration is about you and your partner brand working together and sharing in the ownership of achieving some goals for the marketing partnership that you agreed on. Therefore, you will need to leverage whichever tools make sense to achieve those goals and put them into play. You may start out having conference calls on a casual basis, for example, or an as-needed basis. Down the line, you could be using web conferences that are scheduled in mobile calendars and occur on a weekly basis. You may start out sending monthly manual reports of performance metrics that are relevant to the marketing partnership, and soon after move to a much more sophisticated system that provides username and password-protected access for each individual partner to log-in at a given partner website to obtain those metrics in real time. You may want to email your partner brands your creative assets like logos and messaging that you approve for your program, and at some point create a secured page on your website where those assets live—you just direct your marketing partners to that page to pick up the files. Finally, when starting out you may cut manual checks for payment and snail mail them to partner brands, and somewhere down the line automate that process by transferring the payments every month directly into the partner brands' bank accounts as part of a system that automatically emails the details to the partner brands once the transactions are complete. If you had to pay hundreds or thousands of partners every month, it would certainly be worth automating that process!

You will need to manage your marketing partnership, paying close attention to regular tasks that support the relationship and meet the necessary obligations. Speak with your IT department, whether it's in-house or outsourced, and determine what tasks and responsibilities you can automate to make the partnership run more efficiently. Automation is good, but be sure to have regular communication with partner brands no matter how much or how little you automate and no matter how sophisticated or unsophisticated your partner collaboration tools are. You will want to stay relevant and top of mind. As much as it's nice to have things on autopilot, you need to stay in touch and plan collaboration meetings to discuss new product launches, future initiatives and any training needs.

TRAINING

Your business is your own and your partner brand will need to understand how you operate so that they can engage in smart collaboration with you. As a result, it's important to set aside time for training.

Understanding Your Partner Brand's Needs and Challenges

As I've mentioned a few times now, when you are partnering with another brand, your goal should be to understand their products, services and marketing activities as well as you do your own so that you can maximize the opportunities for success in your marketing partnership. It's a pretty common-sense move, but you'd probably be amazed by how many brands fall short of ensuring that they provide the necessary training for each other concerning everything from their products to how they go about selling them.

With today's technologies, it's pretty simple to set up training programs for your partner brands. You can use web conferencing, and share training presentations online or even post information about your products for partner brands and prospective partner brands on sites like slideshare.net, for example. If you want your partner brands to acquire the competencies necessary for them to market your products and services, you need to provide them with the needed training to get up to speed. And don't forget that just as your partner brands should provide you with insight on how they plan to market your products and services, you should provide them with feedback and share best practices and success stories from what you have done with other partner brands.

Training your partner brand is typically viewed as a 'last step' or 'nice to have' if time permits, but you should ensure that training does occur in a timely manner and is not left behind. Otherwise, this sets the stage for training sessions to be treated as an informal practice that's often pushed to the side because there is no time. Schedule your training sessions, whether they be on-site or by way of web conferencing; it's not good enough to send your partner brand information on your products and hope that they read it. They likely will glance at it and move on to promoting the offer without getting the full scope of what your products or services can really do for their clients.

Building a Partnership Marketing Program

Being a great partnership marketer is not about being an expert in direct marketing or brand marketing or online marketing, but rather about having a general understanding of the many types of marketing strategies and practices that brands use today. With a basic understanding of how these areas of marketing work, you can do what you're good at doing: leveraging assets to create synergies between your company or brand and the partner brand to help your company meet its sales and marketing objectives. It's not about being great at sales or being a superstar social media marketer. It's about leveraging what you need to build the program.

You are a synergy expert and have an understanding of how customers are segmented and targeted, what digital and offline channels are used and which brands (based on their proposition and market standing) would be best for you to work with considering your goals. You have learned what your customers are looking for by coordinating with those that look after customer relationship management and have gained insights as to what the competition is doing to keep their customers happy. You know that you want to add value to your proposition and give your customers something more than the competition, and you are going to leverage whatever it is that you have to get another brand engaged in enhancing your brand and products to do so.

It's an expensive undertaking to try and be all things to all people, so know this: as a brand you can mean more to your customers in their daily lives (whether they are individuals or businesses) than you currently do by making your proposition available elsewhere, by piggybacking on another brand's marketing activities to make another proposition stronger, or by strengthening your own brand by adding value to your offering. What good is a laptop computer without Internet service? What good is the iPhone without applications? Why would you purchase a 50" LCD HD flat panel satellite TV to watch your favorite sporting events if you are not going to sign up with a provider of HD programming? What good is a grocery store that does not carry your favorite brand of cookies? Why would you purchase a home insurance policy from a given provider if you can get the same coverage at virtually the same price from a competitive provider who has also partnered with the loyalty program that you are a member of—whose currency you value—and they are offering you twenty-five thousand points if you take out a policy with them? Why would you rent a car with one company over another?

The partnership marketing program is worth building because it enhances the customer experience by bringing brands together that the end customer likely has a need or desire to engage with.

MAXIMIZING ECONOMIC OUTCOMES

As discussed in chapter 4, it's critical that you have a strong ECP if you want successful partnership marketing programs that yield positive results for both brands and bring the continued economic value that you both are looking for. Maximizing the economic outcomes for your partnership marketing program will depend on your ability to put some key controls in place for the partnership.

The Top Five Controls to Maximize Economic Outcomes in a Partnership Marketing Program

1. Identify the key players in each of the necessary organizational departments that you will be working with and integrate them into the marketing partnership program early and often.
2. Assign responsibilities and design a 'program flow' diagram to ensure that all have been mapped out in terms of who is doing what and when.
3. Ensure that everyone clearly understands what they need to do and when.
4. Develop a checklist for your program to ensure that all of the necessary key players have been communicated with and are OK with what you are doing, so that you will know when you can move forward.
5. Have weekly meetings before, during and after launch to ensure that all is flowing well and you are good to go.

It's not about transactional selling, it's about creating value through a strategic affiliation. If you are focusing on 'selling' your partner, you will not succeed because you will likely fall short of following these key principles that make up your strategic partnership:

- Remember, a marketing partnership should leverage the partner brand and their assets and create an opportunity to truly enhance your partner's offering in helping them to provide their customers with better products and services.

- Don't think of your marketing partnership as a shorter-term 'tactical' initiative. Also focus on longer-term strategic initiatives and programs that will provide incremental value.

- Ensure that you are fully committed to the partnership, to helping your partner meet their sales and marketing objectives.

Finally, take a look at your competitors and see how they are working with partners. Try to deconstruct the programs that appear to be working well for them and try to emulate them. In Canada, Sobeys (a leading grocery chain) recently took on the Aeroplan Miles Loyalty reward program as an incentive for customers to come back to them. One of their competitors, Metro, had been working with Aeroplan's big competitor, AIR MILES, for many years and it appeared to be a good partnership, so Sobeys figured they'd get into the loyalty game as well.

What to Change in Order to Maximize Economic Outcomes

Marketing Channels

I have seen many partner marketing programs go wrong and partner brands become very much disengaged because the 'marketing channels' that were being used were inappropriate in the first place or failed to deliver. I recall one case in particular where a major professional business association that we will call AZZA for the sake of this discussion had a partnership marketing program. They were offering special discounts on various products from several vertical categories and communicated the discount offers to their members on their website. In one particular case, they partnered with a major furniture brand and communicated a compelling offer online, but after a few months they found that it was seriously underperforming.

After further investigation, the association decided to test the program and had a few of their staff and several external parties take advantage of the offer. Their findings were pretty remarkable. Because the partner brand had chosen to use their call center as the marketing channel by which orders for their product would be taken from AZZA members, the program did not gain any traction. Most of the call center agents were not even aware of the program that was being offered to AZZA members, and those who were, were not properly briefed on the discounts available. Dealing with call centers located in remote parts of the world is one thing, but not having them recognize the promotional partner offer that you are calling in for is another thing.

It was obvious that the call center was not capable of dealing with the numerous requests for special offer pricing that were coming from AZZA members. In the end, AZZA learned that if you are going to obtain a great special discount offer for your members or customers from a partner brand and communicate it, you need to ensure that the partner brand can deliver and fulfill on their end; otherwise, it will simply result in a bad reflection on you and the association you represent. My educated guess on this one was that the program was very significant for the association and not as significant for the partner brand, and as a result the partner brand failed to invest in it properly, brief their call center and ensure that the offer was well communicated internally.

'Significance' of the partnership is a key indicator for how engaged or disengaged your partner brand will be. It's definitely not good if they don't consider you to be significant, but rather a 'nice to have' partnership. Like any personal relationship, the partnership should be mutually significant to go off without a hitch and ensure that high levels of partner engagement exist.

The Offer or Discount

Another way that the program can fail to meet expectations and have partner brands become disengaged is when the offer or discount on the product is weak or not any more compelling than the end customer can get elsewhere, such as by buying direct from the partner brand or via any other third-party channel, for that matter. I've personally come across scenarios where affinity marketing programs have offered fifteen percent discounts to members for purchases for certain products and services from a partner brand and I've been able to receive twenty-five percent on that same product when shopping in the partner brand's own store. I've heard of cases where member clubs are offering better discounts on prescription drugs than the coverage a given health insurance company provides for that very same bottle of medication. I've owned coupon books that have a better offer on a given product than that same brand is offering through a major credit card loyalty partner program.

In this digital age, it's hard to be discreet about offers or discounts. Consumers can search online for competitive offers for products and social networking sites like Facebook have enabled consumers to communicate offers to their friends or communities in seconds, creating an uncontrollable force of discussion around your brand, which could be either positive or negative for your organization, depending on the outcome. As a result, it's more important that brands be careful about where and what discounts or offers they make available, and if they are in a program that is meant to be offering something truly compelling, that they deliver on it. Managing multiple offers from different brands requires that you get creative. Don't always settle for the cash or percentage discount. Try encouraging the brands to bundle products together, offering 2 for 1s, incentive purchases or even creating new products with new offers to support a given program.

Before defining your business's priorities you need to ensure that you have a snapshot of what is currently happening in your business so that you can effectively build a partnership marketing program that produces better results. Not all partnership marketing programs are created equal. Without having a read on your current business, you will be setting yourself up for failure and that failure will only result in you not meeting your strategic marketing priorities.

How to Increase Your Chances for a Successful Partnership Marketing Program

1. Get a handle on your key metrics and ensure that your program is aligned to those of your partner brand.
2. Profile your best customers and ensure that your partner brand's program will acquire those same types of customers for you—and that you are not wasting your time going after potential customers that will not buy from you and not remain loyal to your brand for the longer term.

(continued)

3. If you have an existing partnership program or a set of programs that work really well and are driving revenue for your company, try to identify what it is about those programs that's working well for you and determine if there are some variables in place that you can emulate and model your new partnership marketing programs after.

4. If you don't have an existing partnership marketing program or set of programs in place, then take a look at your other marketing programs and determine if there are some variables in place that you can emulate and model your new partner programs after.

5. Use the knowledge that you have gained from your best performing marketing partnerships to create new partnerships with brands that have similar customers and operate in similar horizontal categories and in similar types of verticals.

Little Fish Versus Big Fish

Are you afraid to be the 'little fish' in a marketing partnership and be perceived by end customers as having an offering with very little value compared to your partner brand, the 'big fish'? Well, that's almost always bound to happen when you enter into a marketing partnership with a company that's much bigger than you are. When you partner with a heavyweight who is more visible and essentially more powerful than you are, the prospect of working with them can be quite exciting, but at the same time it poses loads of risk. I'm not just speaking of the risks regarding how much or how little importance your large partner brand gives to the marketing partnership that they have with you. I'm speaking of the perception that the end customers of the partner brand will have of your products and services. If your partner brand doesn't think you are all that important, it will reflect in how they market your proposition and the chances are high that their customers will regard your brand as not all that important either. As a result, you are best to avoid the 'big fish-little fish' scenario if you think you'll be treated less respectfully, and ensure that you get fair market value from your marketing partnerships and take certain things under your control before you launch.

It's up to you to get fair market value from your marketing partnership. For example, don't be bullied into providing exclusivity to a given marketing partner in hopes that they will build your business for you. Microsoft didn't do that for IBM. If they fall short, so will your business and you will not be able to partner with any other brand. Exclusivity for your product with an offer to a certain marketing partner is only a good idea if the exclusivity warrants it. By that, I mean that if a marketing partner can deliver more than the sum of multiple partners for their category, and working with just them allows you to benefit from their size, brand awareness and customer base and is strategic in the sense that you could be blocking out one of your major competitors, then it's worth considering. If that isn't the case, you may be signing away your marketing opportunities to a channel that will underperform compared to the total market that is available to you.

Be sure to understand the partner brand's category, the key players and what percentage of market share each has. Develop an understanding of how the partner brand plans to deliver results for you and commit them to targets and goals that you want to see from them, as they must earn that exclusivity and reward you for it accordingly. Finally, think about the possible 'upside' to your deal in working with the large corporation. What is the 'future value' of the marketing partnership and are you tied in for a very long period of time, even if it's not working well? Working with large corporations can be exciting, but at the same time can limit you from engaging with the available market for marketing partnerships for your products and services. Don't sign any partner agreements that have you locked in for too long and that are not based on both parties meeting their respective goals and objectives.

Make sure that you receive a fair share of co-branded elements. Don't discount your brand completely. Larger brands may like your offering and want to throw it in as a free value-add for their customers, but you need to stand up for your brand and ensure that you are present in marketing vehicles and are not completely invisible. It may be that your partner's brand stands out more than yours does, and in most cases that's OK—especially if they are communicating the offer to their customers—but don't disappear altogether. Placement in key marketing vehicles is crucial. You may achieve a fair level of co-branding on a box that ends up at the end customer's house, but be sure that you have placement on the brand's website or in digital marketing vehicles as well. Not every one of the customers is going to redeem the offer you will be making available and you can benefit from that visibility and awareness and even drive traffic back to your site.

Furthermore, who is controlling the messaging? Be sure that if you are not controlling the marketing messaging for the offer that you at least get to approve it. Wording can diminish your proposition and hold your brand back from creating the right impression. For example, if you are promoting a premium service as a value-add to a partner offer, you want to be seen as a premium service. Be sure that you can at least sign off on the messaging before it's finalized. Include yourself in that process and insist on seeing and approving everything before it goes live on the Web or in print. You may be the little fish in the deal, but your goals and objectives for the program are just as important as those of the big fish.

Know Your Partner Brand's Motivations

Some brands believe it's crucially important to work only with a turnkey solution. They have a comfort in knowing that what you are offering to them in terms of a partnership will not eat up a lot of their resources and time and preoccupy them with something that is new and untested. It's important to consider this when structuring the partnership, because if a vast majority of the key deliverables and obligations fall on the partner to make the partnership successful, you might be in for a very long year ahead.

Other brands are keen to recognize the transactions or 'sales' as part of their business. If they are looking to increase the number of transactions, then chances are that they want those additional transactions to appear on their books and not the partner brand's. They may have a need to recognize the revenue and, as a result, it's crucial that they have the relationship with the end customer, even if you are ultimately supplying the product or service to that customer on their behalf. You may prefer to collect the revenue, have the partner brand drive that customer back to you, and have your brand interface with them and realize the transaction, but as the old expression goes . . . out of sight, out of mind!

Partner brands that are collecting back revenue share from sending you customers, and don't record their own transactions and own their end customer relationships, still may be willing to 'partner,' but if it's outside of their standard practices and operating procedures then you will have to ensure that your company is very visible in the transactions and performance of the program. If not, the partner brand might almost forget that you are involved and you risk not getting the program off the ground because of a misunderstanding and impatience in collecting significant revenue back from you. I cannot stress enough how important it is to know your partner brand in advance of launching the program.

SMART COLLABORATION FROM OTHER VIEWPOINTS

Integrated Marketing Services

Allison Welker, executive vice president of client services at Integrated Marketing Services, says that "marketing partnerships help their clients to meet their objectives. Often what they need the most help with is navigating and understanding opportunities with partner brands. Getting through the discussions, negotiations and managing execution is what most brands struggle with and is where an agency can help." Having said that, here is how Welker answered some questions I asked her:

Q: Why would any brand want to partner?
A: They want to share costs. They also may have a product in the market that needs the visibility in a certain time frame that they can't get on their own and want to maximize that opportunity by partnering. Another great reason is that aligning with the right partner brand can help close the gap and build a brand's image should they have such an issue. Also, some brands have limited

distribution in a marketing channel and by partnering with another brand, they gain access to the distribution opportunities that they would not have on their own.

Q: How do you determine what are the right partner brands for one of your clients?

A: Typically, we like to determine what naturally aligns with or take a look at what is being purchased with the products that our clients are selling. Once we have identified those items or brands, we seek out the ones whose demographics align—as well as the brand essence and messaging—and see if there are appropriate linkages between the two. We work primarily with consumer brands, so we like to align brands that would be found in the same target audience 'shopping basket.' We work with syndicated and retailer data to identify what else is selling through with our clients' products and that gives us a lot of insight into the shopping patterns.

Q: What do you do to get your client engaged in the partnership opportunity?

A: What we first remind our client of is that they need to be open to a variety of different partner opportunities, as you may not always get a deal with the one at the top of your list. I like to refer to the partner development process as a 'continuous courtship' and I encourage my clients not to be set on one brand because you may find out that the one you wanted initially is not necessarily the one to help you meet your objectives. We run our process and try to match our clients with brands that have complementary objectives and are looking for common opportunities. Our first step in the process is to identify the partner brand prospects, followed by step two, which is our 'due diligence' effort and the building of the story for our client and the prospect partner brand, and then we move to step three, which is presenting the opportunity to each brand, getting alignment and initial negotiation.

IGN Entertainment

Chris Ellis, a managing director at IGN Entertainment based in the U.K., thinks that partnership marketing is important because "it's good marketing and cost-effective and should be key to every online business and their growth strategy." According to Ellis, "if done well, with the right audience fit, and right partner, partnership marketing can deliver significant incremental customers and traffic in a very cost-effective manner. The Web has changed the nature of marketing partnerships dramatically." Ellis goes on to point out that "website traffic is often the goal for online businesses worldwide . . . Content swaps or barter deals that on one hand drive traffic and brand awareness will almost just as importantly improve the number of back-links to a brand's website and, therefore, the SEO link equity for the website so that they appear more highly ranked in natural or organic search results on search engines like Google or Bing, for example."

Ellis says that, "a good partner relies on two specific skill sets: business development in getting the deal and marketing to promote the partner brand offers once the deal has been signed. Fall short in one of those areas and it's all for nothing." In order for smart collaboration between partner brands to occur, if a deal does get signed, Ellis says that you must structure your deal in a way that fairly rewards and incentivizes the other party to deliver whatever the metrics for success are, and you need to lock down the marketing and distribution commitments up front. Ellis advises that "if you rely on working in good faith or best efforts, then you are taking a huge risk with your partnership . . . Be specific and ask for placements in store or on a website and promotional commitments up front." Finally, Ellis says, "smart collaboration allows for marketing partnerships to be flexible and change over time because not everything you do at first will go as planned . . . there needs to be flexibility and collaboration between the partner brands to make it work right."

When it doesn't go well, you need to get together with your partner and discuss it. A good partner brand will tell you how they're feeling. If they don't, you must ask them continuously for feedback and create an environment where they feel comfortable telling you why it's not going well for them. A good practice is to get together with your partner brand regularly following the launch of your marketing partnership and see if you can check off a response to the following two questions.

Checklist for Ongoing Review of Your Marketing Partnership

1. *I believe that the value my brand has received from this marketing partnership*
   - ❑ Has helped my company beyond our core competency
   - ❑ Has created valuable synergies for my company
   - ❑ Has helped us to be innovative
   - ❑ Has helped us to provide better service to our customers
   - ❑ Has helped us to penetrate new markets
   - ❑ Has helped us to overcome competitive situations

2. *I believe that the value your company has received from this partnership*
   - ❑ Has helped your company beyond your core competency
   - ❑ Has created valuable synergies for your company
   - ❑ Has helped you to be innovative
   - ❑ Has helped you to provide a better service to your customers
   - ❑ Has helped you to penetrate new markets
   - ❑ Has helped you to overcome competitive situations

Once you have gone through the exercise above, write up some thoughts around how you and your partner brand plan on improving the marketing partnership, as exemplified here:

How we plan to improve performance in our marketing partnership

_____

_____

_____

How you plan to improve performance in our marketing partnership

_____

_____

_____

WHEN IT'S TIME TO END A MARKETING PARTNERSHIP

Smart collaboration should be the goal, but what if you don't get there? My experience is that every marketing partnership has a shelf life and, unfortunately, some partnerships come due earlier than others. You may try your hand over and over at collaborating and working with your partner to achieve the goals and objectives you set out for your marketing partnership, but at some point you will find that you are spinning your wheels and not getting anywhere. That is the point where you have discussed the issues ad nauseam with your partner brand but nothing is changing, but find that you still can't move forward to get what you need from it, and it's really time to consider 'cutting the cord.' Here are some of the reasons to part ways, if you can't collaborate any longer:

- Unable to resolve the conflict
- Have tried to make it work, but results are not changing
- Partner not living up to expectations
- Company (yours or the partner brand's) has changed focus or direction
- Not economically connected

• • •

If you are finding that your marketing partners are no longer giving you the transparency you need and are non-responsive or wasting your time with indecision, then it's likely a sign of things to come. Smart collaboration requires effort, commitment and the flexibility to change where and when necessary. It's picking up and moving forward with a new strategy when the existing one no longer applies and creating efficiencies and best practices around what's worked really well so that you can apply those in the future. Speaking of the future, our world is changing and moving in directions that were unimaginable just ten or fifteen years ago. Our next, and final, chapter will discuss the future of partnership marketing.

8

Partnership Marketing—A Look to the Future

A SHIFT TO DIGITAL IN PARTNERSHIP MARKETING

Let's face it: Our opportunities are limited without collaboration. If what has transpired over the last while from a marketing standpoint continues to take shape, then our need to collaborate will only increase. The decline in print advertising and an increasing tendency to put more marketing dollars, resources and energy toward online and digital platforms have created more opportunities for partnership marketing than ever before.

Essentially, partnership marketing as a discipline and practice within small businesses or large organizations is still very new. As a result, it hasn't yet found a home in many marketing departments. However, over the past twelve years, I have spotted a trend: More positions are being created in partnership marketing and more-traditional marketers are now taking on partnership marketing roles and responsibilities. Businesses are continuing to expand their focus in this area as the value of partnership marketing becomes more apparent to them. The cost-effective nature of partnership marketing and the excitement created by the commercial synergies that link brands together to meet their sales and marketing objectives is more attractive than ever.

In addition, in the digital age, partnership marketing is now easier to implement. According to Mike Burnette, director of partnership marketing for Meredith Corporation, "the business world is rapidly increasing their digital footprint and partnership marketing will be no different." He goes on to point out that "the digital landscape makes the implementation and execution of marketing partnerships much easier than before and partnership marketing activities will grow more rapidly in the digital and online channels than in non-digital or offline programs." Burnette is seeing this firsthand: Over the past couple of years, there has been a shift in digital channels for his business. According to Burnette, "Meredith is already transacting thirty-five percent of marketing partnerships online, whereas a few years ago, we were not doing any partnership marketing online at all."

It's fair to say the shift to digital is here to stay, whether we like it or not. Particularly in the U.S. market, the shift to online classifieds, coupled with the meltdown of the housing market and the shake-up of the auto industry, has hurt publishers of newspapers and their ability to derive the revenues they once did from advertising support, to the point where many of them are reducing the number of publications they produce or are even going out of business altogether. The subscription side of their business (the other major source of revenue) is also hurting, because younger readers are flocking to digital sources for their news and entertainment, thus dragging down newspaper subscriptions. In October 2009, the Audit Bureau of Circulations reported that average weekday circulation plunged by 10.6 percent compared with the same period a year earlier (the six-month period ended September 30, 2009).

- If consumers or businesses are not willing to engage with content in the way that they used to, and certain industries are looking for ways to reinvent themselves and align with what their customers want, then how does partnership marketing play a role in all of this, and what can it do to become an integral component of what many brands turn to in the midst of this digital shift?

- How can you leverage the principles and practices of smart collaboration to ensure that your brand stays ahead of the competition and keeps existing customers loyal for longer?

In most cases, you need to do more with less: You cannot afford to spend as much as you once did. At the same time, you need to drive revenues for your business, and forming long-lasting collaborations with the right partner brands is an effective way to meet this challenge. Brands such as Ford and Microsoft, for example, are already successfully doing just that. They have teamed up to create a product called SYNC, a factory-installed system that they developed using the Microsoft Auto platform. SYNC allows drivers of Ford vehicles to combine their digital life with life on the road. According to the Ford website, "SYNC is an easy-to-use in-car connectivity system, standard on all 2010 Lincoln models and available on select 2010 Ford and Mercury models. SYNC allows you to operate most popular MP3 players, Bluetooth-enabled phones and USB drives with simple voice commands." It goes on to describe the features of SYNC, which include

- Turn-by-turn navigation
- 911 Assist
- Vehicle health report
- News, sports and weather
- Real-time traffic reports
- Business search

The website also notes that "Ford and Best Buy have teamed up to help you choose the right phone to get the most out of SYNC. That's why Geek Squad tests the compatibility of the mobile phone with SYNC's great hands-free features and awards the phone a rating of Advanced, Standard or Basic."

The above example illustrates how a brand such as Ford recognizes that, in the future, consumers looking to purchase a new car and businesses wanting to lease a fleet of cars for their employees will be searching for new kinds of features, such as those that SYNC provides, in those vehicles. Ford stepped up to the challenge and partnered with Microsoft to develop a unique solution to power their vehicles with technologies that customers want and that could sway their car-buying decisions.

How will you do the same? How will you integrate partnership marketing into your business so that you are offering value-adds to your products or services that keep you on trend and help you sell more?

According to Internet marketing firms such as HubSpot, "marketers who spend fifty percent of their lead generation budget on inbound marketing channels report a significantly lower cost per sales lead than those who spend fifty percent or more of their budgets on outbound marketing channels" (HubSpot, *State of Inbound Marketing Report*, February 2010).

Outbound marketing typically refers to the practice of a brand sending messages out to their target audience by using the following:

- TV spots
- Print ads
- Cold calls
- Email blasts
- Trade shows

Inbound marketing typically refers to tactics and strategies that are used by brands to increase the potential of being found by customers:

- Blogs
- Whitepapers
- Viral videos
- Podcasts
- Webinars
- Feeds and RSS

The report goes on to demonstrate how the average cost per lead for outbound marketing-dominated brands that they studied in 2009 was $332, while inbound marketing-dominated brands' average cost per lead was just $134, or sixty-one percent lower. It's an interesting trend: More and more brands are shifting larger portions of their budgets to inbound marketing activities such as blogs, social media, podcasts, SEO and pay per click (PPC) campaigns. SEO is the process of editing the content of a website, including the HTML coding and making references to specific keywords, so that the website is prominently listed in the top search results for those keywords when they are entered into the search box of search engines like Google. PPC is an Internet advertising model whereby advertisers only pay the website that is displaying their ad when the ad is clicked on. They are doing this because inbound marketing costs less.

And partnership marketing costs less, too. Partnership marketing is essentially inbound marketing through your partner brand, leveraging their marketing assets and competencies to drive customer acquisition for your brand. Just as a majority of inbound marketing activity is now happening online, so, too, will partnership marketing activities, and they should prove to be just as, if not more, cost-effective than other inbound marketing campaigns.

Collaborating with others or 'sharing' your marketing in the new digital world is quicker, cheaper and easier than before. It's also less labor intensive: You will do much less work to market your products and have much more to gain at a lower cost. Think of SYNC: How much more labor intensive and costly would it have been for Microsoft to go into the auto business and install these systems in vehicles themselves, instead of co-marketing with Ford and having the car company make SYNC available as a factory install? Ford can generate product leads and sell the product better than Microsoft can, because they already sell vehicles and their accessories. It's an example of smart collaboration, the kind of partnering that can transform brands like Ford and Microsoft into new product categories and establish them in spaces they are not typically known for.

ASSOCIATIONS WILL GIVE MORE VALUE TO MEMBERS AND PARTNERS

In the future, associations will need to team up with partner brands so that they can deliver more to their members. At a minimum, associations will be looking to retain their current membership, but the ultimate goal will be to increase their numbers. Whether those associations are professional, behavioral, religious or cause-related, or appeal to members based on a given life stage, they will be looking to add value to their membership and give members a reason to keep paying their dues. They will also need to stretch a bit, and give more to their funding partners as well. There are some exceptions to this, of course: Some professional associations, such as those serving practicing doctors, lawyers and accountants, for example, won't need to actively seek new membership, because their members are obliged to continue paying their dues in order to practice within their given professions, and thus their associations need not worry about marketing to them. For the most part, however, associations will face membership-retention issues as membership levels start to drop. They will need to partner with complementary brands and provide their members with more services, member discounts and unique and compelling content that enhances their value proposition and makes members realize that they are losing out on something should they not renew their membership.

Associations will need to demonstrate more value—beyond the media and placement that they traditionally give—to sponsors or partner brands that feed the other stream of revenue (aside from the dues) that keeps associations working. They will need to tap into their member base and provide more opportunities for partner brands to sell and market their products, engage with sponsors on a deeper level to give them opportunities to provide exclusive content for the association, and work with them strategically to uncover new concepts that leverage non-traditional vehicles for sponsorship that allow for increased brand exposure. Essentially, associations need to do more to produce better results for their partners and give them more commercial value, and enhance the program to provide a performance component in which economic value is derived from new customers and sales transactions and the partnership is more than simply a branding exercise.

MORE COMPETITION IN RETAIL

Marketing partnerships with retailers will be harder to develop and, for those that already have them, much more difficult to maintain. The emergence of private label and white label or store brands, coupled with the fact that more and more retailers are entering the manufacturing arena, will make it difficult for traditional, premium brands that have leveraged retail as a distribution channel for their goods and services in the past to maintain the sales and margins they once enjoyed. Take a closer look at where the retail sector is heading and what the future looks like. Will brands be able to occupy the same amount of shelf space as they once did? Will they be able to compete price-wise with in-store brands? Will they still benefit from the in-store co-marketing programs they once received? These questions are not limited to the grocery retailers; we can ask them of electronics, furniture and health/wellness categories as well. What was once easily accessible territory, owned solely by premium brands, is disappearing fast, and has been for years. This makes it even harder for established premium brands to maintain their presence, and far more difficult for new premium brands to get into stores at all. Of course, there are exceptions to this rule—products such as Apple's iPod or Proctor and Gamble's Tide maintain their prominent placement in stores because consumers expect to see them on the shelves and because, although they have competitors, they are not suffering as much as some of the other premium brands.

As a result of all this upheaval, premium brands will have to do a lot more to corner that sought-after retail shelf space. Some companies are coping by buying the shelf space, supporting in-house or third-party loyalty programs with a 'points offer' and giving retailers special pricing on products to create bundling opportunities in which a discount is passed on to the end customer for purchasing a bundle-pack containing, for example, three products at one special price point. Brands that are looking to maintain or even get into retail (especially in the case of start-ups looking for distribution) will need to become more creative and explore every possible angle the retailer has to partner with them. In a nutshell, established brands who now face more competition from in-house brands will have to evolve their relationships and move from transactional-based distribution relationships to full-fledged marketing partnerships that leverage several marketing assets, including store flyers, in-store demonstrations and mobile couponing.

Many retailers are 'multi-channel' these days. They offer products to their customers in-store, online and even over the phone or through a catalog. One of the channels may work better for your product or service—many new brands, for example, vie for space on a retailer's website and take advantage of drop-ship options, much like Amazon.com's seller central program. The retail store is still, however, where the majority of customer transactions occur, and thus your product needs to be on a shelf and be 'seen', if you want to maximize profits.

If you're looking for mass distribution, be prepared to support retailers by advertising in their flyers, integrating into their loyalty programs and even paying for shelf space. Often it's better to start small, and test out a few independent retailers that may be willing to sell goods on consignment or who can promote your service in-store to their customers, before trying to establish a partnership with a national chain. By giving the small, independent retailer a special offer and having them generate leads for your product, you can handle the transaction and sale and save the store that work. This approach can be quite effective if you are selling a service as opposed to a product.

LOYALTY PROGRAMS WILL EXPAND

Loyalty programs will continue to provide brands with opportunities to acquire and retain customers, because coalition partner programs will expand far beyond what is on the market today. Miles, points—whatever the currency is—will provide more ways to access programs as a consumer and provide more opportunities for partners. B2B incentives will become a larger focus for the large loyalty-program providers. They will continue to emerge and offer brands and their customers rewards for purchasing products from them.

We will also see more opportunities on the mobile loyalty front (loyalty coupons that can be scanned on a mobile phone, instead of paper coupons); more creative programs emerge in health, well-being and environmental sectors. Brands such as Starbucks, for example, have tested out mobile coupon programs in which two-dimensional bar-coded coupons are sent to the customer via partner offers in text messages. Brands will offer mobile loyalty programs to customers, and retailers will become more equipped with software that reads the coupons directly from mobile phones at the point of sale, thus giving customers the opportunity to receive discounts anytime, anywhere.

Finally, we will see an emergence of proprietary loyalty programs where brands can drive consumers to their website to register for an account and accumulate points (or another form of currency) to eventually redeem for rewards from the brand and their partner brands. Huggies Diapers, for example, are doing this by including stickers in their packaging that are marked with a numeric code. As a customer you can go to their loyalty program website and register by providing your name, email address and date of birth and entering the numeric code; Huggies then assigns a number of points to your account. Once you accumulate a certain number of points, you can redeem them for a coupon that will be sent to you for a free pack of diapers. You can then take the coupon to retail partners of Huggies to get your diapers. They have also partnered with brands like the Gap, where you can redeem your accumulated points for a Gap gift card. We will see more of these proprietary programs emerge in years to come as the ability to launch them in this digital era is easier than ever, and more and more consumers are comfortable with the process on going online, entering their data and joining these programs.

GREATER USE OF ONLINE CONTESTS AND SWEEPSTAKES

Online contests and sweepstakes can generate leads, users and traffic for your website. Offering these programs to existing customers is a good strategy if you are looking to increase engagement with your brand, products and services, but offering them to a partner in return for placements and visibility in their website is an even better strategy. If you can build a partnership in which you co-brand a contest and drive users to register on your site, it can be quite a cost-effective tool for user acquisition. Make sure you partner with a site that has the users you're seeking—those who will take interest in what you are offering. If you sell computer hardware, for example, don't run a contest that targets nurses' association members—it's not a great strategic fit. If you sell watches for health-care workers, however, then nurses would be a great target.

Overall, more brands will be looking to align their promotional tactics with partners that market to their target audience. You will see an emergence of this trend and brands leveraging it not only on their websites but also in their social media channels and networks. They will also focus on smarter, better and more effective placements of contests and offers.

USE OF GEO-TARGETING IN PROMOTIONS

Geo-targeting solutions—messaging consumers with a 'promotional message' when they are within one kilometer of your store—will allow retailers to take advantage of nearby traffic. It's like having someone stand on the corner a block away from your store and hand out coupons to passersby. Partnerships with mobile companies and the development of applications to enable this strategy will become increasingly important. The benefits are potentially enormous, and time-saving, too—no more designing and printing up coupons. Certainly a more environmentally friendly solution.

Partner brands of retailers could also leverage co-marketing opportunities to promote coupons for certain products and use them as short-term promotional blasts to help boost sales during slow periods or during given times of the year. Brands such as PayPal have created mobile payment systems for iPhone, Android and BlackBerry, so that customers can pay bills directly from their mobile phones. It's only a matter of time before the major credit card brands jump on board as well. VISA is already working on a mobile payment platform of their own, for example. Merchants will need to embrace this new reality and partner with companies like PayPal and VISA to offer their customers more payment options.

SMALL BUSINESSES WILL PARTNER WITH LARGE CORPORATIONS

Another emerging trend is small entrepreneurs partnering their brands, products and propositions with large corporations. Many recently downsized employees will resurface with newer, fresher ideas and exciting ways of moving forward in the coming years, including all sorts of opportunities for partnership marketing. Partnerships will form between smaller, lesser-known companies and larger corporations, enabling all those who once worked for large corporations to now tap back into the products, services and infrastructure that the large corporations offer and leverage them to acquire customers for their new employers. Consultants will further leverage their ability to partner with large companies through the emergence of more collaborative partner networks that enable small-business owners to effectively market products and services as channel partners, without incurring the costs or expending the resources to do so.

Brands like Cisco have launched initiatives such as Partner Marketing Central, which supports partners' continued development in their marketing of Cisco products and will help them in their co-marketing strategies and programs. With a growing need for the Cisco partner network to leverage their websites and social media networks, Partner Marketing Central lets partners co-market with Cisco. It's a huge change from showing partners how to market to actually enabling them and providing the tools and content to co-market products. Partner Marketing Central also has a module called Event Center, which provides their partners with all of the necessary modules to execute events. The Event Center has applications like social media tools so that they can run an in-person or online event. Any Cisco registered partner can take advantage of Partner Marketing Central for free, making Cisco more partner friendly than ever.

PRODUCT PLACEMENT WILL EXPAND

Another emerging trend is that of product placement. We've seen brands leverage television programming and movies already, but soon we will see this type of branding move into other types of art and visual media as well. Increasingly, brands will start to claim spots in music videos; we are already seeing this happen in Lady Gaga videos—*Telephone* is filled with product placements for Virgin Mobile. And it will happen more and more. As artists look outside of their record labels for the necessary funds to build their brand, they will turn to corporate organizations with deep pockets that are shifting their spending from traditional advertising and looking for new ways to reach customers and new audiences.

Our smartphones and portable gadgets will harness the power of more and more applications and functionalities all the time. The iPhone has well over two hundred thousand applications, including ones from Starbucks, CNBC, ESPN and Bank of America. Amazon recently introduced an application for Facebook, in which friends can tell other friends what they would like for their birthday. Amazon facilitates the purchase by integrating within the popular social media site, collecting the data and then processing and fulfilling the order. Microsoft is also working with Facebook to incorporate their Bing search engine, so that users can conduct Internet searches without having to leave Facebook.

Slideshare

Rashmi Sinha, CEO and co-founder of Slideshare.net, says that she leveraged the Web as the platform or vehicle for building Slideshare, a service that allows users to share slide presentations by posting them on the website so that others can easily view them on demand. Since the company's launch, its website has had over seventeen million monthly visitors and fifty million page views. Slideshare's user-acquisition strategy is to leverage blogs, search engines like Google, social media sites like Twitter and other online networks to drive users to the site and get them to sign up for an account, where they can upload their slide presentations and make them available for sharing. Unlike businesses that are built on the creation of applications for the iPhone or iTouch, and that use Apple's platform as the vehicle for their growth, Slideshare wants to become a destination site.

Sinha and her team at Slideshare also created Slideshare for LinkedIn to "fulfill the need for business professionals who use the popular social network to leverage their ability to share their presentations with their professional networks," says Sinha. She further explains that Slideshare did not want to build the professional network, but, rather, wanted to provide LinkedIn with a strong partner value proposition that their users would benefit from. Slideshare already had success with this model on Xing.com, which is the European equivalent of LinkedIn. "Platforms like LinkedIn have evolved," says Sinha, and "now require more tools for their users and members." According to her, a small percentage of new-user acquisition is generated from Slideshare through these programs, but the primary purpose is not to acquire new users, but to engage the users that already use the service so that they use it even more and share with other connections on LinkedIn. "As sites like Facebook and other social networks become more of a commercial or B2B play, we will look to partners and collaborate with them as well. It's all about increasing reach and usage."

PocketCocktails

Dee Jones, president and co-founder of PocketCocktails.com, an iPhone app company, started the business in June 2008 with her husband. Jones always wanted to have her own company, but for a long time did not know where to focus her entrepreneurial efforts. Her husband was working in publishing in a family business. The couple (based in Toronto, Canada) had begun to notice a shift in the traditional publishing market, with book publishing costs elevating and returns diminishing. The iPhone launched in Canada in June 2008 and they bought one a month later. They loved using the device and were intrigued by the many downloadable applications available for it. They also liked Apple's platform, and soon taught themselves to create applications that they could make available to other users via the Appstore.

Soon, PocketCocktails.com was born. Jones loves to entertain and create mixed drinks and cocktails, and figured that other iPhone users would benefit from her fun drink mixtures and lively application. Jones saw the business opportunity and jumped on it. She quickly learned that there were three ways she could market and generate revenue from her application: sell it for a set price, say $4.99; make the app available free of charge, and sell advertising to generate revenue; or dive into partnership marketing—partner with an established brand and integrate them into the application.

Jones chose the third option: She signed a deal with Grey Goose, a popular vodka brand that loved her app. Since Jones was a Grey Goose customer already, she welcomed the concept with open arms. She changed the word 'vodka' to 'Grey Goose' in all relevant recipes and provided the company with placement within the app. In return, Grey Goose paid for its product's placement.

Most iPhone applications are free to download—about sixty percent of them, according to my unscientific estimates. And it's simple to create an application for iPhone. You pay a nominal fee to become a developer, submit forms, and wait for your application to be approved. Still, with over two hundred and fifty thousand downloadable iPhone apps available, it's hard to get noticed. That's why Jones is always promoting and marketing her app to bartenders and other interested people. "You can't just create an app, you have to market it," she says. Jones has also worked with Grey Goose to promote her app; it has been leveraged in some Grey Goose marketing vehicles. Leveraging those vehicles and her partnership is much more cost-effective than advertising in trade publications. She agrees that their advertising is targeted to iPhone users, but also notes that an advertisement in trade publications is quite expensive and may not generate as good a return on investment as Grey Goose.

Finally, Jones believes that the entire app world will soon be "heavy into marketing partnerships." She thinks that most apps will be heavily sponsored, with messages that drive people to storefronts or to websites, where they can buy products and take advantage of special offers.

AN EMERGENCE OF PUBLIC-PRIVATE PARTNERSHIPS

We will soon see an emergence of government-corporate, or public-private, partnerships, such as the well-known ENERGY STAR program, which is a joint program between the U.S. Environmental Protection Agency and the U.S. Department of Energy. ENERGY STAR helps consumers save money by promoting energy-efficient practices and products to them. Thousands of popular brands have partnered with ENERGY STAR. Samsung, for example, places the ENERGY STAR logo on several of their products, which brands them as being ENERGY STAR compliant. We will see more of these partner programs, which assign a given standard or seal of approval to a product because it has met the qualification criteria, in different vertical categories. Increasingly, consumers will want to know more about their products—not only where they are made, but how the products fit into their lifestyle and whether they help make the world a better place.

Cause-Related Partnerships

We will also see more cause-related marketing partnerships between brands and charities. For example, Home Depot promotes their support for Habitat for Humanity, and FC Barcelona supports UNICEF, sporting their logo on the team's jerseys instead of a corporate logo. The emergence of social media and other interactive marketing tools will allow more brands to tap into this conversation with their customers, followers or users, and thus gain a better understanding of the causes that are important to them. They will then use this knowledge as a basis for creating cause-related marketing partnerships with organizations that resonate with their user base.

• • •

I hope you now have a better understanding of where partnership marketing seems to be heading. The channels will change, the partner programs will evolve as our technology and ability to innovate evolves, but the fundamentals will remain the same: Partnership marketing means partnering with the right brands that target the right audience, in order to provide a strong value proposition to your partner and to the end customer, and thus create value from your program. The opportunities are endless. You can partner with a few key brands or many. In the end, however, what will matter is that you choose the right brands to partner with based on the many principles and practices discussed in this book.

Let me know what you are up to with regard to your partnership marketing programs as well as your thoughts on where you think this exciting and dynamic space is heading. Email me at ron@geysermarketing.com or check out my blog, at http://geysermarketing.wordpress.com. Let's keep the conversation going!

Glossary

Acquisition channel—a marketing channel, such as direct mail, leveraged to acquire a new customer

Added-value marketing partnership—like a distribution marketing partnership, but with a true and unique value add, typically in the form of a gift with purchase, for the end customer that they can't get anywhere else

Affiliate marketing network—a network of brands who reward each other for directing customers to their respective businesses; the network manages, monitors and supports affiliates in their activities

Affinity marketing program—a program with special offers on products from partner brands, promoted by the affinity group seeking to add value to their existing customers, members or donors

Average number of transactions, or ANT—a calculation of the total number of transactions for a given week, month or year for a given business, divided accordingly to get an average number of transactions per day for the period

Average transactional value, or ATV—a calculation of the value of all transactions divided by the number of transactions by customers on a weekly, monthly, quarterly or annual basis

B2B—business-to-business marketing

B2C—business-to-consumer marketing

Bounty revenue model—a payment program whereby one brand provides a one-time fixed fee payment to another

Brand extension—the practice of taking a well-developed brand name into a different category and spinning it off, e.g., Virgin started off in music and moved into travel and mobile communications

Brand fit—the ability to share common brand values and attributes

Brand value—the market value for a given brand

Bundling—pairing a product together with another product

Co-branded—a form of marketing program whereby a single product is associated with more than one brand name, e.g., the Motorola Droid mobile phone from Google and Verizon

Co-marketing—a scenario whereby both partner brands are leveraging separate distribution channels and their own marketing style to market a new product that they have created together

Content marketing—using various marketing activities that allow for the sharing, creation and promotion of content, in an effort to engage current and potential customers

Cost per acquisition, or CPA—the total cost of acquiring a new customer for a business

Cross-marketing—the act of marketing products or services that are complementary to yours to your customers and vice versa

Customer relationship management, or CRM—the strategy and process a business will use to engage, nurture and interact with customers

Customer segmentation analysis—an analysis illustrating the different customer groups that a brand may sell their products to

Customer touch point—a vehicle that engages the customer with a brand, such as a call center, invoice or e-newsletter

Distribution marketing partnership—a marketing partnership whereby the secondary partner brand markets products of the primary partner brand to their customers

Economic connection as partners, or ECP—the ability of partner brands to drive economic and commercial value for each other's businesses

End customer profiles—a description of the types of end customers, including socio-demographic and behavioral characteristics, a company or brand sells to

End customer value proposition—the value and benefits that the marketing partnership is bringing to the end customer

Geo-targeting—used in Internet marketing to determine the geographic location of a website visitor so that the website can display location-specific content

Horizontal market—a market that meets the needs of a wide variety of industries, such as computers

Inbound marketing channel—the tactic or strategy used by a brand to get found by their customers

Key Performance Indicator, or KPI—measures that brands use to determine how successful they are at achieving their marketing goals and objectives

Lifetime value—the present value of the future cash flows attributed to a customer relationship; some partnerships will generate a higher lifetime value from customers than other partnerships

Loyalty program—a structured program that rewards customers for buying products

Marketing channel mix—the mix of channels that are used to market a product, such as partnership marketing, direct marketing, customer relationship marketing and online marketing, determined by the frequency and use of each

Marketing collateral—the assortment of new and traditional media used to support the sales of products or services, such as packaging, printed brochures, white papers, ads, flyers, vouchers and coupons

Marketing value chain—in partnership marketing, this refers to the target audience, brand objectives, campaign development and measures of a given partnership marketing program

Marketing vehicle—the program, tactic or strategy that a brand uses to market their products

Metric—in marketing, this refers to a system of measuring a campaign and its effectiveness, such as responses, sign-ups, transactions, page views, customers acquired and time spent online

Mobile loyalty—leveraging mobile telephony to engage customers and create loyalty to a given brand, such as by offering mobile coupons, incentives and contests

Offline—marketing to customers using non-electronic tactics and strategies

Opportunity cost—in partnership marketing, this is the cost of partnering with the next-best brand when you can't partner with your first choice, e.g., the opportunity cost of partnering with Subway would be Quiznos and vice versa because you may only be able to partner with one

Outbound marketing channel—the tactic or strategy used by a brand to send messages out to their target audience

Partner collaboration tool—a partnership management software that allows for collaboration and effective management of the marketing partnership

Partner pitch deck—the presentation used by a given brand to pitch their value proposition to a prospective partner brand

Partner value proposition—the value and benefits of your partnership to the partner brand

Partnership marketing asset—a marketing asset that will be leveraged in a marketing partnership, such as a brand, audience, customers and marketing vehicles

Pay per click, or PPC—an Internet advertising model whereby advertisers only pay the website that is displaying their ad when the ad is clicked on

Point-of-sale materials, or POS—materials typically used in retail environments to engage customers in the store

Primary market research—tried and true research methods that are customized or tailored to a brand's needs

Primary partner brand—the brand that the secondary partner brand is promoting to their customers

Product enhancements—improvements and innovations made to a product to improve its marketability and product lifetime value

Proof of concept—a demonstration of a program, concept or theory as it's been put into play and proven in a market

Proprietary—content that is marketed under the exclusive rights of its owner

Sales traction—the ability to attract sales

Search engine optimization, or SEO—the process of editing the content of a website, including the HTML coding and making references to specific keywords, so that the website is prominently listed in the top search results for those keywords when they are entered into the search box of search engines like Google

Secondary marketing research—using data or information that was already collected in studies by given agencies, consulting practices or governments

Secondary partner brand—the brand that is promoting the primary partner brand to their customers

Small and medium-sized businesses, or SMBs—an acronym that groups small and medium-sized businesses that typically have less than a hundred employees

Sponsorship marketing—known as trading cash for branding on a given property, such as Aflac does with NASCAR

Turnkey—a type of solution or program that needs no customization and is ready for use in its current form

Value proposition—the value and benefits that a given partner brand can deliver to another

Vertical category—a list of categories defined by industry and specialized need for products and services that relate to their area of business, such as financial services, travel, auto, banking and publishing

Vertical market—a market that meets the needs of a very specific industry, such as a software platform created expressly for mortgage-related products in the consumer banking industry

Warm transfer—the process of transferring a customer from one brand's call center to another brand's call center to engage that 'warmed up' customer in new products or services from the partner brand

White label—also known as private labeling, this is where one company produces a product for another company that then markets the product as if they made it themselves

Index